KU-632-074

THE ROUGH GUIDE to

MySpace

by
Peter Buckley

1st Edition

ROUGH
GUIDES

www.roughguides.com

Credits

The Rough Guide to MySpace

Text, design and layout:
Peter Buckley
Contributing editor: Sean Mahoney
Proofreading: Liz Carter
Production: Katherine Owers

Rough Guides Reference

Series editor: Mark Ellingham
Editors: Peter Buckley, Duncan Clark,
Tracy Hopkins, Sean Mahoney,
Matt Milton, Joe Staines, Ruth Tidball
Director: Andrew Lockett

Publishing Information

This first edition published November 2006 by
Rough Guides Ltd, 80 Strand, London WC2R 0RL
345 Hudson St, 4th Floor, New York 10014, USA
Email: mail@roughguides.com

Distributed by the Penguin Group:

Penguin Books Ltd, 80 Strand, London WC2R 0RL
Penguin Putnam, Inc., 375 Hudson Street, NY 10014, USA
Penguin Group (Australia), 250 Camberwell Road, Camberwell, Victoria 3124, Australia
Penguin Books Canada Ltd, 10 Alcorn Avenue, Toronto, Ontario, Canada M4P 2Y3
Penguin Group (New Zealand), 67 Apollo Drive, Mairangi Bay, Auckland 1310, New Zealand

Printed in Italy by LegoPrint S.p.A.

Typeset in Avenir, Minion and Myriad to an original design by Peter Buckley and Duncan Clark

The publishers and author have done their best to ensure the accuracy and currency of all
information in The Rough Guide to MySpace; however, they can accept no responsibility for any
loss or inconvenience sustained by any reader as a result of its information or advice.

No part of this book may be reproduced in any form without permission from the publisher
except for the quotation of brief passages in reviews.

© Peter Buckley 2006

240 pages; includes index

A catalogue record for this book is available from the British Library

ISBN 13: 978-1-84353-842-4
ISBN 10: 1-84353-842-3

1 3 5 7 9 8 6 4 2

THE ROUGH GUIDE to

MySpace

by
Peter Buckley

www.roughguides.com

Contents

Introduction viii

About this book x

Part 1: The basics

1. The big picture 3
everything you ever wanted to know
about online communities

2. The networks 13
MySpace and beyond

3. Your set-up 25
from broadband to browsers

4. Common concerns   **37**
don't believe the hype

Part 2: Welcome to MySpace

5. MySpace FAQs   **49**
the burning questions

6. Your first time   **59**
getting started

7. Searching & browsing   **77**
where to start

8. Making friends   **83**
breaking the ice

9. Mail, comments & chat   **91**
it's good to talk

10. Groups & forums   **103**
something for everyone

11. Events & calendars   **107**
save the date

12. Blogging   **111**
welcome to the blogosphere

13. More MySpace   **117**
last but not least…

Part 3: Make it your own

14. Pimp your Profile   123
it's all in the code

15. 15 top hacks   135
make your MySpace stand out

16. Images & photos   147
getting images online

17. Video clips   157
movies and MySpace

Part 4: MySpace Music

18. Artist SignUp   169
building a band profile

19. Making music   177
get the most out of your recordings

20. More music   183
the MySpace music page

Part 5: Playing it safe

21. Avoiding trouble   191
socializing safely on MySpace and other communities

22. Dealing with difficulties 199
where to find help

Part 6: MySpaceology

23. MySpace weirdness 209
stranger than fiction

24. MySpace resources 215
websites & blogs

Index 222

Introduction

why a book about MySpace?

The Internet has always been about communities, and in the last few years the most cohesive type of online community yet has evolved. Within these communities – such as MySpace, Bebo and Friendster – every user has their own homepage, or Profile, where they can posit thoughts, receive messages from other users, showcase their music and, most importantly, link to the homepages of their online friends and acquaintances.

These new-generation community sites – often labelled social networks – have grown at an astonishing rate and have taken on many roles: a hangout and flirt zone for teenagers, a stage for musicians and comedians, a networking spot for professionals, a drop-in for new parents, a soap-box for politicos … the list goes on.

Whether you're new to online communities or a long-standing user, this book has something for you. The first section examines the whole phenomenon, provides the low-down on the most popular sites, and gives practical advice to get you started.

From then on in, the book focuses primarily on MySpace, the biggest online community of them all. However, much of the information given – such as the basics of HTML code, and advice on preparing digital pictures, music and video for use on the Web – is applicable to every community site, so even if you're not a MySpace user you'll doubtless find plenty of useful tips.

Peter Buckley, September 2006
www.myspace.com/roughguidetomyspace

About the author

Peter Buckley is the co-author of several best-selling Rough Guides titles, including *The Rough Guide to the Internet* and *The Rough Guide to iPods, iTunes & Music Online*. He has contributed to countless other Rough Guides as an editor and designer and is also the host of Rough Guides' successful Podcast series (www.roughguides.com/podcasts). Peter also pens fiction and as a signed-up MySpace Artist gigs and records regularly with several Brighton-based bands.

Acknowledgements

The author would like to thank everyone at Penguin and Rough Guides, especially Ruth Tidball, Tracy Hopkins, Joe Staines, Matt Milton and Duncan Clark for their support, help, and for making the whole project such fun. Special thanks go to Sean Mahoney and Andrew Clare for their contributions and wit, and also John Duhigg and Andrew Lockett for giving the project the green light. Several big shouts go out to all those MySpacers and friends who've kept me going while I wrote this book, especially Ginger Lee, Birdengine, Pine Forest, Euchrid Eucrow, Natasha Khan, Abi Fry, Lizzy Carey, -A+M, Davidddddddddddd, Jonathan Buckley, Sam & Helen, Rupert, Jess and not forgetting my Dad.

This one's for Rosalie ☺

Part 1

The basics

The big picture

everything you ever wanted to know about online communities

This book will help you get the best from MySpace and other online community sites. It will also undoubtedly spruce up your homepage or Profile and aid you in navigating your community's complex avenues safely. But coming to an online community such as MySpace for the first time can be a daunting experience. So, before we get into the meat and potatoes of how everything works, let's address the many questions that you have probably already asked yourself. This is also the

the basics

section of the book that will help you if you really don't know the first thing about the subject, or if you perhaps need to untangle a few facts from the maze of hype and myth that has sprung up online and in the wider media.

The basics

What is an online community?

Online communities such as MySpace are many different things to many different people, but the simple answer is that they are websites. More specifically, they are websites designed to foster communication and friendship. They're a bit like a mixture of school yard, social club and notice board. They are somewhere you can chat and interact with your regular "real world" peers, but also befriend individuals from all over the world.

Is a social network site the same as an online community?

Yes. Some sites prefer the former term and others favour the latter. But neither is that popular with the majority of the users. Ask the average teen if they are a "social networker" and you will more than likely be rewarded with a blank stare. Ask them if they are on MySpace, and you'll be pointed in the direction of their personalized homepage (also known as a "Profile" page).

How many online community sites are there?

There are hundreds of community websites on the World Wide Web. Some are specifically aimed at professionals, others cater for college students; many are vast in their scope (like MySpace) and boast populations larger than some small nations. To find out the specifics of a few of the more popular sites, turn to p.13.

Are online social networks a new thing?

In the big scheme of things the whole Internet is a relatively new phenomenon, so yes, they are a new thing. It can all be tracked back to 1995, when a social networking website named Classmates.com appeared on the scene. Similar to the UK's Friends Reunited (which was born a few years later in 2000), its aim was to help people locate and keep in touch with old friends from kindergarten, school and college. This site is now widely recognized as the model for the online community sites that followed in its wake. In the US, SixDegrees.com began in 1997 and Epinions in 1999, while

on the other side of the Atlantic Ciao.com, Dooyoo and ToLuna all started their respective networks in the late 1990s. In 2002 Friendster was launched; still one of the more popular sites, it

was among the first to employ the notion of a "Circle of Friends" in its structure. In the last few years many more sites have been launched, with MySpace, Bebo, Facebook and Google's orkut among the most successful. Through the contagious power of word of mouth, these networks have expanded and evolved at a staggering rate, so despite their relative infancy, they are rapidly becoming a dominant force in the cyberworld.

Tell me more about the "Circle of Friends".

While sites such as Friends Reunited and Classmates.com primarily nurture relationships based on a shared history, such as school attendance, the "second generation" sites like MySpace, Bebo and Friendster rely on the internal dynamics of a group of friends to grow in size. Think about the way any of these sites will have started. The founding member of an online community website sets up a homepage and emails all his friends asking them to join. They accept, create their presence on the site and then invite all their friends to join, who in turn invite their friends, etc, etc. Pretty soon the whole world seems to know about it.

Which network is for me?

For most people the choice of network is easy – they go for the one all their friends are on. End of story. But don't feel that you have to limit yourself to just one. Though it can become a logistical nightmare of email juggling and password confusion, many online community users will have one group of friends on Bebo, for example, and another crowd on MySpace. This is, of course,

the basics

much the same as in the real world, where we often separate family, work or school pals and "weekend" friends. You might also find yourself drawn to a particular community because of your interests – MySpace, for example, has long been associated with musicians. But even in this instance most fresh account holders will have followed their crowd to get to the registration page.

For a more comprehensive overview of the online communities you are most likely to encounter, turn to p.13.

Tell me more...

How do online communities work?

As mentioned earlier, most online communities rely on the dynamic of a "Circle of Friends" to sustain themselves. If none of the individual community members ever contacted each other or made fresh connections, then the community would be little more than a list filed away on a Web server somewhere. To encourage their own propagation, sites make features such as homepages, blogging tools, viewable friends lists, messaging tools and online address books available to their members.

Are they exclusively online affairs?

By no means. Many community websites are online networks that directly mirror real-world communities. Facebook is a good example. It has become a very popular site with US school and college pupils, to the point where many official student groups are now represented online. Also worthy of note is MySpace Music's strong association with the real world. Not only do many

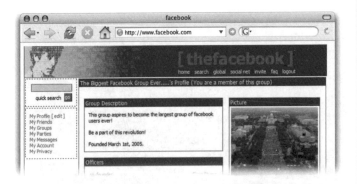

record labels use the site to spread the word about their releases and hunt for new talent, but on a local level, its "comment" and "messaging" features are regularly used to arrange concerts, band practices and gatherings. There is, of course, a flipside to all of this. Though frequently exaggerated by the media, the real-world dangers posed by stalkers, bullies and paedophiles do exist and should be taken seriously; they are covered in far more detail later in the book (see p.37).

Can anyone sign up?

Most of the social networks on the Internet are public, allowing anyone to join. However, each individual site usually has its own "user agreement" which may well contain specific rules and regulations – most commonly relating to a minimum age restriction and the uploading of offensive or copyrighted material – which you have to sign up to when you join. This being the Internet, the policing of such regulations is an entirely different matter.

This above all: to thine own self be true…

Do I have to use my real identity?

In terms of your online persona there is very little to stop you creating an alter ego for yourself online. On MySpace, for example, there are even those who have hijacked the identities of fictional comic book heroes and characters from Shakespeare plays (pictured). More sinister are those instances where individuals maliciously create profiles using other people's names in order to ruin their reputations, or create false identities to disguise dubious activities. For all your burning questions relating to the darker side of social networking, see p.37.

Do I have to pay to sign up?

Most online communities are completely free to join – which is one of the reasons why they have become so popular with teenagers and young adults. Sites such as MySpace are almost exclusively funded by the advertising that litters much of the screen real estate; and given the volume of traffic that passes through most of these sites, you can bet those ads generate big bucks. You might, however, stumble across some sites that have "premium" accounts you do pay for, which offer additional services or dispense with ads altogether. Be sure you know exactly what you are paying for before you sign up.

If you do have a little extra money burning a hole in your pocket, you could perhaps decide to spend it on a digital camera or some flashy image software to help improve the look of your Profile (see p.34).

What do I need to join?

More often than not, all you need to get involved in an online community is an active email account (see p.29), a means of accessing the Internet and plenty of free time.

What am I likely to get out of it?

That really is up to you. If you open an account and then just sit back and wait for other people to search you out, then you're likely to be rather disappointed, rather quickly. If, however, you embrace the tools at your disposal and put in the hours, social networking can be fun, enlightening and confidence-building – as well as a great way to make new friends.

How many people are signed up?

In the larger online communities, there are tens of millions of so-called "active" accounts. MySpace, for example, reportedly sees something in the region of 200,000 new accounts created each and every day, and has an overall population of more than a hundred million members.

Of course, a significant number of the reported overall figures can be attributed to "dead" accounts, which have been abandoned by their creators, but not deleted. But this should in no way belittle the significance of such communities. Early in 2006 it was reported for the first time in the media that MySpace, only two years after its inception, was receiving twice the traffic of search engine Google.

What kinds of people are they?

Good question. The networking phenomenon is still relatively young and definitive studies are few and far between. However, it is fair to say that social networking has found its largest market in young adults and teenagers. More interestingly, statistics relating to MySpace that appeared in March 2006 showed that the gender split of the community's population was about as close to 50/50 as it could get. For the full story, visit: www.micropersuasion.com/2006/03/myspace_mania.html

> **Tip:** For the most up-to-date population statistics visit: en.wikipedia.org/wiki/List_of_social_networking_websites

02

The networks

MySpace and beyond

I f you're wondering which online community is for you, the short answer is "as many of them as you want". You don't have to align yourself with just one. Many teenagers and adults alike maintain active accounts with various networks to stay in touch with different groups of friends. Equally, you might make your choice based on your interests: musicians, for example, historically settle at MySpace. And there are even sites out there for pre-teens and, umm, dogs. This chapter takes a comparative look at a handful of the most important sites on the Internet.

MySpace www.myspace.com

▶ **Population** 106 million registered users
▶ **Demographic** 14–35 years old

With over a hundred million registered users to date, MySpace is by far the most populated of all the online social networks. Over the course of just fifteen years, the Web has evolved from being a place of complete obscurity into the most incredible communication system the world has ever seen. In that time, many major online companies have come and gone, so what's stopping MySpace from going the way of the dodo?

Well, as we discuss throughout this book, the site's flexibility of design and freedom of content makes it a tempting option for anyone who truly wants to express themselves online.

Like all of the major social networks, MySpace allows you to store and share photos (see p.147), access or upload music (see p.167), search for friends (see p.79), mass-mail everyone in your online address book (see p.93), join groups (see p.103), post videos (see p.157) and write blogs (see p.111). MySpace has also seen a revolution in the way people are using Web design and HTML code (see p.123), thanks to its fully-customizable Profile pages.

But there are other options out there – lots of other options – and new ones are popping up at an alarming rate. And with each new offering, improvements are made and networks are rarefied. However, with such diversity comes a certain lack of accountability. Whereas larger, better-known sites such as MySpace, Bebo (see opposite) and Friendster (see p.16) are having to tackle online safety issues in response to public outcry, many of the less "visible" sites are responding more slowly.

Bebo www.bebo.com

▶ **Population** 22 million registered users

▶ **Demographic** 15–24 years old

Bebo's home office may be located in San Francisco, but uprooted Englishman and Bebo CEO Michael Birch seems intent on dominating the rest of the Anglosphere before mastering the New World. With its clean interface, 1MB photo limits and uncomplicated video uploads (including a point-and-click method of linking to

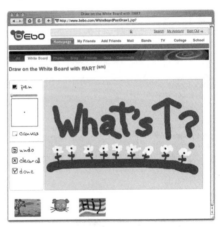

Bebo's Message Board commenting system lets you leave friends hand-drawn communiqués.

YouTube videos), it won't be long before Bebo is challenging more established sites for their American users.

The site has all the expected social networking tools, including customizable "likes" and "dislikes", links to friends via their universities or secondary schools and extremely malleable "skins" (page themes). You can also create and participate in polls and quizzes, blog your daily deeds and use instant messaging (IM) through Skype. Within Bebo Bands, "friends" are automatically changed to "groupies", signed acts can converge on their label's page and thirty-second teaser tracks can be posted as downloadable MP3s.

Friendster www.friendster.com

▶ **Population** 27 million registered users
▶ **Demographic** 21–30 years old

The grandaddy of the social networking scene – although it's only five years old – Friendster is the original phenomenon on which all other massive online communities have based their success. At its inception, Friendster was so popular that even in its unofficially released (beta) state, there were close to a million new users signing up each month. As the first of its kind, and with such an easily manipulated monicker, it's since spawned copycat sites such as Hatester, Enemyster and Introvertster, as well as a slew of unreal and mostly funny user accounts known as "pretendsters" or "fakesters".

Once Friendster released its official version, it stripped the fake accounts (to the dismay of many users) and added TypePad blogging services, video posting supported by Grouper and a music "jukebox" powered by Pandora. All three of these additions offer easy-to-use and powerful file manipulation options: TypePad provides a full range of page layout, commenting and archiving features; Grouper enables one-click posting and provides video editing tools; and Pandora helps you set up your own online radio statio. Friendster also supports groups and forums – handy for finding HTML code tips so you can improve your homepage's appearance (see p.123) – and has a classified section listing job openings, items for sale and housing.

Never mix business with pleasure

Online communities aren't just about staying in touch with distant friends. All the major networks encourage meeting new people, sharing ideas and establishing contacts, but within such large frameworks it can simply be too time-consuming to find precisely who or what you're looking for. If you're on a mission to expand your address book or meet local singles, you can streamline the effort by joining sites specific to your goals.

Below, on the left, is a list of business communities where you can find and talk to people in your own industry and share your résumé with potential employers. On the right are dating sites, each one with its own unique clientele, from hipsters to homosexuals to hotsteppers.

LinkedIn www.linkedin.com
Ryze www.ryze.com
ZeroDegrees zerodegrees.com
ecademy www.ecademy.com
openBC www.openBC.com

Make Out Club makeoutclub.com
Social21.com www.social21.com
Matchdoctor matchdoctor.com
MatchActivity matchactivity.com
DowneLink www.downelink.com

the basics

Facebook www.facebook.com

▶ **Population** 8 million registered users
▶ **Demographic** 15–24 years old

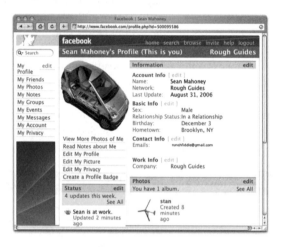

Based on the American college practice of giving directories of student photos and profiles to incoming first-years, Facebook has helped continue the fine tradition of senior students identifying fresh meat (and all that may imply). It's not all fun and games, however. Facebook can be very handy when organizing group events, be they high-school, college or business based. You can also post relatively large photo albums, each containing up to sixty photos at 4MB a piece, and you can update those albums straight from your mobile phone. And while there's a definite advantage to Facebook's "closed community" arrangement, the badge creator helps you make online business cards that can be viewed from any website.

Go to the head of the class

Online communities can form around any fascination or fancy, from knitting to engine repair to foot fetishes. But one of the most popular common bonds is a shared education. Accordingly, there are quite a few social networking sites based on school ties. These sites allow current students to discuss homework assignments and stay in touch during the holidays, while generations of alumni can share stories of Sister Bernadine rapping their knuckles with a ruler. MySpace includes school groups within its vast framework, but if you want a less music-and-dating orientated online experience, try exploring the following options:

Friends Reunited www.friendsreunited.co.uk
A UK-only network with highly specific search criteria combing every level of education, work history and military service so users can trace and contact old friends. The success of this site spawned sister sites Genes Reunited and the unabashedly nepotistic Friends Reunited Jobs.

Classmates.com www.classmates.com
Touting over forty million users among its country-specific sites (including its forays into Germany and Sweden with www.stayfriends.de and www.stayfriends.se), Classmates.com is one of the oldest and most visited "reconnection" sites in the world.

myYearbook www.myyearbook.com
Intended for current students, myYearbook encourages study groups, gives members "locker space" to house files and doles out gold stars for excellence.

sconex www.sconex.com
Not sure if that guy in your chemistry class is really making eyes at you? Just find his sconex page and add him to your list of "crushes". He'll be anonymously alerted, and if you end up on his crush page, you'll know the feeling is mutual.

The Student Center www.student.com
Started as a discussion board over ten years ago, The Student Center now offers user pages, contests, games and quizzes, a poetry centre, an advice board, yearbook and photo albums, a "hot or not" ratings channel and links to state-specific teen sites throughout the US.

Yahoo! 360° 360.yahoo.com

▶ **Population** 2 million registered users
▶ **Demographic** 18–35 years old

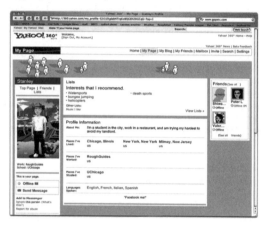

An immediate advantage of Yahoo 360° is the way it smoothly integrates itself with established Yahoo email accounts – you can quickly connect a new 360° page to all the contacts in your Yahoo address book, and you won't need to spend any time establishing a profile or "avatar" (personal cartoon representation) if you've already filled out the same fields in Yahoo instant messaging (IM). Among its page personalization options are user-created or downloadable themes, a music, movie and book review section, quick posting thought-bubbles called "blasts" and an area dedicated to your favourite RSS feeds (see p.116). You can also blog to your heart's content, and then use the embedded RSS feed creator to automatically alert friends to new posts.

orkut www.orkut.com

- ▶ **Population** 27 million registered users
- ▶ **Demographic** 15–30 years old

The Google corporation is known primarily for its Web search engine, but a click-through to their "Google Products" page reveals a sprawling list of both on- and off-line software – including desktop photo organization (Picasa, see p.35), product price comparisons (Froogle), and Excel-style spreadsheets accessible from any computer connected to the Internet (Google Spreadsheets). So it should come as no surprise that Google has a social networking site in its arsenal. At the time of writing, orkut is only available as a beta (unfinished) release, and you won't find any way to gain network access of your own accord. Instead, as was the case with the Gmail beta, you'll need to be invited to join orkut by a current user.

In its beta state, orkut offers meagre page personalization features – you can upload images and create small photo albums, and that's about it. Orkut lacks video and music capabilities, there's no

blog integration and you're limited to the layout provided by the site. In addition, the "invite only" system has spawned a black market of sorts, where current members sell invites for upwards of $10 on eBay.

21

the basics

hi5 www.hi5.com

▶ **Population** 50 million registered users
▶ **Demographic** 18–30 years old

Popular all over the world, but with a particularly large following in South America, hi5 boasts a user base nearly twice as large as its nearest competitors (though that's still less than half the population of MySpace). While dedicated band sites aren't as well supported or as heavily cross-linked as on some other networks, musicians can still upload and share their original tracks, and any user can listen to a wide range of popular music with the hi5 Musicplayer – each track is also conveniently linked to the iTunes music store. Profile pages can hold up to 2500 photos at 5MB a piece, meaning users almost never need worry about re-sizing images.

Second Life www.secondlife.com

▶ **Population** 600,000 registered users
▶ **Demographic** 18–30 years old

This is the first of a new breed of online community. Second Life is, in fact, a variation on the Massively Multiplayer Online Role-Playing Game (MMORPG) genre made popular by titles like EverQuest and Ultima Online. But instead of hunting for treasure and battling demons, Second Life is a world constructed in a way very similar to our own, ripe with property developers, numerous artistic and business endeavours and personal fortunes of varying degree. Users – called residents – navigate the cyberverse using "avatars" modelled after themselves or some fantasy version thereof, and can create houses and other items with building blocks known as "prims". Of course, building objects costs money, especially houses which also require the buying or leasing of "land" from either the site's owners or another resident.

There are both free and paid versions of the service – you'll need a paid version to do anything more than stroll about aimlessly – and membership requires downloading an application that interacts with the world's command centre. Originally a PC-only program, Second Life now runs on Macs and Linux machines, although some options don't run as well as on Windows.

Networks for children and animals

Some networks, such as Club Penguin and Whyville, tout themselves as youth-focused educational sites, purporting to teach children online etiquette and the value of money within a child-safe environment. Whyville even requires its users to pass a test for a "chat licence", quizzing them on proper responses to potentially dangerous chatroom queries. Both sites use filters to block foul language – with Whyville even going so far as to alert a moderator when "suggestive" words or phrases are used (like "pants", or "what's your phone number?") – and don't include any image posting options. Instead, children can create online cartoon representations of themselves called "avatars", and spend most of their hard-earned virtual loot customizing their appearances.

Another children's site, Imbee, creates a more visible online presence for children, allowing them to post blogs and upload pictures, but it counters potential predation or grooming by limiting interaction to parent-approved associates. Imbee requires credit card identity verification, and grants parents publishing approval for all blog posts, messages and pictures.

Club Penguin www.clubpenguin.com
Whyville www.whyville.com
Imbee www.Imbee.com

Apparently making new friends online no longer requires a set of opposable thumbs. Many animals maintain their "own" sites on pet-dedicated networks, with pictures and profiles listing everything from favourite toys to best tricks.

Dogster www.dogster.com
Catster www.catster.com
Petster www.petster.com
HAMSTERster www.hamsterster.com

03

Your set-up

from broadband to browsers

Most people reading this will already have access to the Internet via a computer of some description. And that's really all you need to get started, though if you are still uding a dial-up connection, now is the time to think about broadband. Yet there are other things to think about. You need tools at your disposal for everything from browsing the Web to editing digital photos. This chapter briefly answers the various questions commonly asked by online community members regarding Internet access, software and computer set-ups.

the basics

Getting online

Is my current computer up to the job?

If you have bought a new PC or Mac in the last few years, then you are undoubtedly ready to go. With an older computer, you may find that your system can't handle anything faster than dial-up access via a standard 56K modem, which is going to make streaming music or video very clunky.

My Internet connection speed matters, then?

The faster the better really. With a basic 56K modem and dial-up connection you will be able to use an online community site such as MySpace, but once you try watching video clips or streaming music from Profile pages, a slow connection becomes very frustrating. Equally, uploading content – especially music and video files – is painfully slow with a sluggish Internet connection.

It's also worth remembering that the providers of dial-up Internet accounts often charge you for each minute you spend online via your phone bill. Social networking can be a time-consuming business, so if you are shackled to a dial-up connection, try to find an ISP (Internet Service Provider) that offers a monthly fixed-rate package with a free phone number.

So broadband is the way to go?

Now that broadband (assuming you can get it) has become far more affordable, there really is no reason to wait. It is, however, well beyond the scope of this book to guide you through the minefield of choices out there. For the full picture, get hold of the most recent edition of *The Rough Guide to The Internet*.

Do I need to worry about usage limits?

It depends what you're going to be doing. Usage limits (also referred to as download limits) are set by many broadband ISPs to cap the amount of data you can shift across your connection each month. If you watch loads of videos or regularly listen to streamed music from community sites, you might be surprised by just how much data you're downloading. And you also need to consider the volume of material you're uploading. You could end up paying through the nose for any excess if your ISP's usage limits are paltry. Even worse, you might find your Internet service suspended until the start of the next month when your ISP's meter goes over its limit.

Contact your ISP to check the exact usage limit of your account. The figure they quote will probably be expressed in

the basics

gigabytes. To give you a very rough idea, listening to around 250 songs on MySpace represents around one gigabyte of data passing through your Internet connection.

What about public access?

In theory, you can log in to an online community anywhere that you can get access to the Internet, whether it be in a cyber café or library, or via a public Wi-Fi hotspot. However, it is always a good idea to find out if the establishment or hotspot you are using has any kind of policy on the matter. Many schools and colleges, for example, are now clamping down on students using their facilities for such purposes.

Tip: If you do ever log in to a site such as MySpace in a public place, you should protect your password in the same way that you might protect your PIN number at an ATM machine. Also, be sure that when you do log in any "REMEMBER ME" or "SAVE PASSWORD" check boxes are unchecked. Finally, when you are done, always log out.

Should I log in at work?

Common sense dictates that if you do intend to surf MySpace, or any other online community, using a computer at your place of work, you should check first with either your boss or the network administrator. Social networking is certainly not worth losing a job over, however desperately you want to deal with that growing stack of new Friends Requests.

Many employers have even gone so far as to block certain sites from their networks. Though you can find ways to work around this online – using systems that employ proxy IP addresses to allow anonymous surfing – it probably isn't worth the risk.

Email accounts

Why do I need an email address?

Taking the example of MySpace, it is impossible to sign up for an account without an active email address. You need to use your email address every time you log in, as well as to keep tabs on Friend Requests and other alerts. It can also be used as a means of blocking individuals from trying to befriend you (see p.88).

Can I use my work email?

Yes, but it might be a bad idea (see p.44). You would be far better off opening up a separate email account that you can use exclusively for handling all your social networking emails.

Where do I go for a new email account?

Email addresses are very easy to come by. The main types of account you'll come across are POP3 accounts from ISPs (you may already have a spare address that came as part of your Internet connection package) and webmail accounts from services such as Yahoo! and Gmail.

Which webmail account should I choose?

Webmail accounts are everywhere, and they are normally free (many major websites will give you one in an attempt to get you to return). Usually they're very easy to set up – you simply log in, give a few details and you'll have an account in seconds.

Microsoft's Hotmail (aka MSN Hotmail) is the most popular. However, with their market domination secure, Microsoft have implemented a policy of freezing accounts that haven't been used for just a few weeks. To reactivate you have to sign up again, and you'll lose all your old messages and addresses – and any mail sent to you in the interim will be rejected. Unless you

pay an annual subscription, this will happen again and again. Furthermore, the free Hotmail accounts currently offer a comparatively small storage capacity.

So if you do want a webmail account, you'd be well advised to look elsewhere – you'll easily find more storage space and a longer "freezing" period. Yahoo!, for example, offer a 1GB account with a four-month freeze. Or you could try a 2GB account from Google Mail – aka Gmail.

Gmail www.gmail.com
Hotmail www.hotmail.com
Yahoo! www.yahoo.com

For thousands more providers of free webmail accounts, browse the following lists:

Free Email Provider Guide www.fepg.net
Free Email Address Directory www.emailaddresses.com

Hardware & software

PC or Mac?

It doesn't matter. Both Apple Mac owners running OS X and those with a PC running Windows can get into social networking and online communities – they are just websites after all. There are a couple of exceptions to this, in the form of online virtual worlds (see p.23) that blur the boundaries between regular community sites and role-playing computer games. If you want to sign up to these, you may need to download some kind of software to get started, which will probably be PC-only.

the basics

Stay up-to-date

Both Apple and Microsoft regularly publish security updates for their respective operating systems, which should be downloaded and installed religiously to protect your computer from viruses and malware (malicious software) on the Internet. If you run OS X, connect to the Internet and click "Software Update…" in the Apple menu. If you run Windows XP, download Service Pack 2 (SP2) from Microsoft (if you don't already have it). This major upgrade of XP includes various security updates and enables the automatic download of all future updates. Equally, if you run anti-virus software, make sure that it is always kept up-to-date.

What other software do I need?

Your Web browser is the key component of your online community toolkit. It's not only the window through which you view the pages that make up your chosen site, but also a package for downloading music and video files from it. Your computer will already have a Web browser installed (unless it's really ancient), but that doesn't necessarily mean it's the best one to use.

Which browser should I use?

It's a personal choice – use whichever one suits you best. Chances are, you currently use Microsoft's Internet Explorer. It's decent enough, but IE's popularity is mainly down to the fact that for years it has come pre-installed on nearly every new PC as a part

Tip: If clicking on any link, image or button on the page of an online community prompts you to download an application, browser plug-in or enhancement, decline – it's asking for trouble.

of Microsoft Windows. At the time of writing, IE lacks many of the features of some of the alternatives, and it's widely considered to present more problems in terms of security. For both these reasons – and because many computer users don't want to encourage Microsoft's monopolisation of the global software market – you should at least test drive something else, the obvious choice being Firefox. That said, by the time you read this, IE7 may have been released, which promises a few significant improvements.

Pre-2005 Macs also came with a version of IE, but the standard Mac browser is now Safari. In most ways, Safari is an excellent browser – especially Safari RSS, which was released in 2005 as part of the new Tiger operating system (OS X v10.4). It's fast, intuitive and nice-looking, with a Google search box built in. It also features excellent tabbed browsing and top-class newsfeed tools. Still, if you use a Mac – and especially if you have the earlier (pre-Tiger) version of Safari – it's worth checking out Firefox to see which suits you better.

What's so great about Firefox?

Released in late 2004, Firefox is an excellent browser created by the Mozilla Foundation. Released as an open-source product, Firefox has a huge range of features, and even if you discover something that it can't do, you'll often find that you

the basics

can easily add the desired function via an extension downloaded from the Firefox website.

Furthermore, most experts agree that Firefox leaves PC users slightly less vulnerable to potentially harmful scripts and other Web-based nasties than Internet Explorer does. With excellent privacy tools and many other handy extras, this is the best choice for PC users (and arguably the best for Mac users) at the time of writing. Download it for free from:

Firefox www.getfirefox.com

What software do I need to edit photos?

Unless you have a really old computer, your system will probably already be able to open most types of image file. But if you want

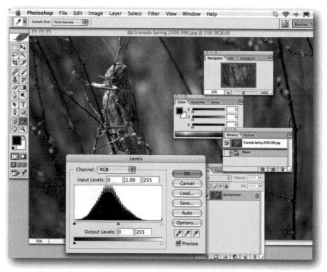

to create, resize or compress pictures for your online community page (see p.151), you'll need some image-editing software.

If you already have a program for managing your digital photos, you'll probably find that it has all the editing and re-saving tools you need. iPhoto on Macs, for example, has decent editing tools and easy export options (select the image you want to re-save and click Export in the File menu). But there are also many image editors available to download for free, from open-source-powerhouse GIMP to the user-friendly Picasa.

GIMP www.gimp.org
Picasa picasa.google.com

As for commercial packages, the professional's choice is Adobe Photoshop, which is great if you can afford it. But there are also many less expensive tools that do nearly as much – Paint Shop Pro being one example.

Photoshop www.adobe.com
Paint Shop Pro www.jasc.com

For help using these packages, try:

PhotoShop Cafe www.photoshopcafe.com (Photoshop)
Pinoy7 www.pinoy7.com (for Paint Shop Pro)

What software do I need to make music to post on my band's Profile page?

Whether you have signed up with MySpace Music, Bebo Bands or another artist-focused community, you will end up wanting to post your own MP3 files to your Profile page. Mac users who've bought their machines in the last couple of years already have a one-stop-shop on their computer in the form of GarageBand (see p.178), part of Apple's iLife media package. GarageBand can be used for everything from recording individual instruments and vocals to mixing, building sample-based music from scratch and exporting music in a web-friendly format. It also boasts additional Podcasting tools. If you don't have it already, iLife can be purchased for £55/$79.

PC users are also well catered for by shareware such as Reaper (see p.178). Audacity also comes highly recommended: it's free, it lets you record and edit MP3 files, and it has loads of built-in effects, multitracking facilities and a very useful unlimited undo feature.

Audacity audacity.sourceforge.net (PC & Mac)
Reaper www.reaper.fm (PC)
iLife www.apple.com/ilife (Mac)

If you have some money to spend, you could give Auqio Sound Studio a try with a Windows PC system; it's a very professional application that costs only £60/$100. On a Mac, the best way to part with your hard earned cash is by picking up a copy of Apple's Logic Express (£199/$299) – one of the professional big brothers of GarageBand.

Auqio Sound Studio www.auqio.com (PC)
Logic Express www.apple.com/logicexpress (Mac)

Another useful tool for converting MP3 files between different bitrates is iTunes, available for both Mac and PC (see p.179).

04
Common concerns

don't believe the hype

Just as the real world harbours dangers around every corner, so does the Internet. And judging by many of the stories that appear in the wider media, more wrongdoers and villains can be found within online communities than anywhere else online. This, coupled with the fact that these communities are primarily inhabited by teenagers – and that most parents are Olympic standard worriers – makes for an explosive situation. This chapter takes a look at some of the questions most commonly asked by parents and by teenagers, and should hopefully separate the fact from the myth along the way.

the basics

What parents ask

What are the dangers?

Despite the fact that, statistically speaking, your kids are put in more peril every day by road traffic than by online communities, the safety issue that has recently captured the limelight is the very real problem of online "grooming". This is the process by which paedophiles attempt to connect with young people on their own level and gain their trust, before arranging some kind of real-world liaison. By creating false online personas for themselves, these individuals can adopt the jargon and gossip of young people in a very sophisticated and subtle way, so they become entirely indistinguishable from a teenager's genuine peers.

Online communities make this process very easy as there are few safeguards to prevent adults from creating deceptive Profile pages, and the amount of personal information that some kids reveal on their own pages can make them very easy to target.

Sounds like reason enough to ban my kids from these communities.

You could try. There are ways to block specific websites from being used on your home computer, but if your kids really want

> **Tip for parents:** Talk to your kids and make sure they know you are at least trying to understand what these social networking sites mean to them. That way, if things go wrong, they are more likely to come to you for help.

> **Tip for parents:** Discourage your kids from revealing too much information about themselves online (see p.62), and investigate the various safeguards the networking sites offer to filter requests for friendship from "unknown" peers (see p.88).

to use these sites, they will find a way. The far more sensible course of action is to talk to your kids intelligently about what they do online and discuss all the dangers with them. Teenagers are not stupid, and they're not looking for trouble, so familiarize yourself with the facts and then make sure they do the same.

Are these sites really that bad?

Like anything else, social networking sites and online communities have both good and bad points. Yes, there are dangers. But these sites also allow teenagers to interact with their peers, be creative and explore their own personalities. Think about what you were doing as a teenager. The main difference between then and now may well be that your parents had no way of knowing exactly where you were hanging out or what you were doing, or what kind of language and attitude you used. Oh, and today's teens are going to come out the other end with Web design and creative writing skills.

Surely online communities are monitored?

Although sites like MySpace put a lot of effort into policing the material and users that fall within their jurisdiction, we are talking about websites with tens of millions of pages, containing content that is updated from minute to minute, 24 hours a day, seven days a week. Like it or not, the responsibility for monitoring these websites ultimately falls to the users and those close to them – their families and friends. Every online community has procedures for reporting offensive material, harassment, identity theft, etc. They are happy to hear from anyone reporting these activities and are sure to delete the offending material swiftly.

Are there any safeguards?

Each online community has its own way of doing things, and you are sure to find an FAQs section on each site that will tell you what you need to know. What's more, things are changing. In June 2006, MySpace was taken to court by the family of a 14-year-old girl who was raped by a fellow site user. The lawsuit stated that MySpace had "absolutely no meaningful protections or security measures to protect underage users". In response, the community has since introduced several new safeguards.

Are my kids going to find pornography?

Very possibly, yes. Though most online communities maintain an active anti-pornography policy, the enforcement of such a stance is very difficult; so it really is up to you, the users, to report offensive material as and when you stumble across it (see p.205).

With regard to kids, those with the necessary skills to create and maintain a MySpace account probably already know that you only need to type the merest hint of innuendo into a search engine to come face to face with porn sites. Most perfectly

> **Tip for parents:** The process of deleting a MySpace account is covered on p.76; for other communities, look for the FAQs or help sections on the site's homepage. NEVER delete your child's account behind their back … whatever the reason.

normal kids will search for a swear word the first chance they get – after all, children are pretty childish – so it might not be long before they encounter a porn merchant, even if they're not already curious about sex.

What can you do about it? Well, you could try using the censoring tools that are built into your Web browser. These filter out questionable material, either by only letting permitted sites through or by banning certain sites or withholding pages containing shady words. However, censoring tools rarely work flawlessly, nor do they fool clued-up older kids and teenagers, many of whom will simply work out how to circumvent them. With older kids, then, it's probably better to talk to them about the issue rather than trying to shield them from it.

You could also try spying on their online activities, by simply clicking on your Web browser's "History" button to see which websites they've been looking at. However, they are probably smart enough to cover their tracks, and talking to them is always going to be better than spying on them.

Is my child too young for this?

There are two questions here really. First up, each community site will have its own rules and regulations about the minimum age of users. On MySpace, for example, you must be at least 14 years old to join. The site's "Terms of Service" additionally state that "if a user is under 18 and misrepresenting their age, the account may be deleted".

If you find your child is an underage member of any online community, work with them to delete the account (without too many fireworks) and suggest a more appropriate site aimed at younger kids (see p.24).

In terms of your child's own emotional development and if they are old enough to belong to an online community, that is something that you will need to come to a decision about within the family. Sites such as MySpace can be fun, but as any parent knows, kids can be hurtful and cruel, and there is no more public arena for bickering, bullying and cat fighting than the Internet.

Even if you suspect your kids are not ready for some aspects of online socializing, making them aware that you understand why they want to be involved and taking an interest in what they are doing means that, if they do need help, they will come to you.

Should kids be spending so long online?

That's really a parenting call. But there are loads of issues that need to be addressed. Is their time online hindering their studies? Are they getting enough exercise? Have they lost interest in their real-world friends or hobbies?

Perhaps the most important issue is whether they are using their online community time productively. Experimenting with web designs (see p.123), writing a blog (see p.111), socializing (see p.83) or creating a band profile (see p.169) can all be very positive experiences; however, numbly "trawling" through sites to kill time is probably not the best use of anyone's evening.

But I read so many horror stories in the paper.

If you only associate online communities with the media circus that surrounds them, you are only seeing half the picture. Talk to your kids and their friends; get them to show you how it works. They are far more likely to accept your words of caution if you are talking to them on the same wavelength.

Privacy

Will all my personal details be safe?

The less information you put online, the less you have to worry about, so don't feel compelled to spill your soul when signing up (see p.62). Equally, most community sites, being free, will never require you to reveal credit card information or payment details (though there are exceptions to this rule, see p.24), and you should never disclose your address or phone number.

That said, there have been reports of phishing on MySpace.

What's phishing?

Phishing is when users of a genuine website, such as MySpace, are lured onto a bogus webpage that exactly resembles those of the site they thought they were on. From there, a login screen might appear, tricking them into entering their MySpace user-name and password (see p.196, for advice on recognizing bogus login screens). While online community users do not typically store financial information on their personal pages, phishers are

the basics

hoping that the login information they collect will be the same for other accounts at online banks and shops etc – which is a very good reason not to use the same password for all your online dealings.

Will being on a site such as MySpace prevent me from getting a job?

There have been many reported instances of people being "checked out" online by both colleges and potential employers, so the way you present yourself on your Profile or blog could perhaps prevent you from getting a job. Similarly, some people have been fired by their employers after their less-than-saintly activities were revealed on social networks. It's worth bearing in mind that the Internet isn't the best place on the planet to unleash whatever venom you may have for your employer.

In short, always remember that online communities are public places, and anything you type and any pictures you post may be read, copied, forwarded and distributed without your knowledge.

Finding help

Someone is pretending to be me online – what do I do?

This form of "identity theft" is relatively common. Though it is sometimes little more than a prank, it can be an extremely vicious form of online bullying. The first thing to do if this happens to you is to get in touch with the administrators of the commu-

Tip: Your Friend ID is a string of numbers that appears immediately after the phrase "friendID=" in the address bar at the top of your browser when logged in and viewing your own Profile page.

nity. In the case of MySpace, they ask victims to send a "salute" – a photo of yourself holding a handwritten sign with the word "MySpace.com" and your "Friend ID" (see above) written on it. This salute is needed to verify your identity. MySpace will then delete the Profile that uses your identity without your permission.

MySpace also has a separate link for teachers being persecuted by false Profile pages.

What can I do about harassment and threats?

Without a doubt, the best thing to do is ignore the person who is harassing you and take whatever steps you can, using the site's systems, to "block" them from making any more contact with you. For the lowdown on how this is done in MySpace, turn to p.204. If the individual has made contact with you outside of the social network or you believe you are being stalked or are in any kind of danger, it is a matter for the police.

Is there anything I can do to protect myself?

There's a whole chapter near the end of this book (see p.191) that tells you exactly what you can do to keep yourself safe while

the basics

enjoying online communities, and there are numerous additional tips scattered throughout these pages.

Who can I talk to?

If you face any kind of problems as a result of an online community or encounter anything that upsets you online, talk to a teacher, your parents or another responsible adult. You may have to explain how social networking works before they can understand the problem. Alternatively, you can look online for help – there's a list of useful addresses on p.218.

Part 2

Welcome to MySpace

05
MySpace FAQs

the burning questions

Many of the most important questions that you have about MySpace will already have been covered in the previous chapters, but here are a few MySpace-specifics that might need clearing up. If you can't find what you're looking for in this chapter, or in the rest of this book, look online. MySpace has a reasonably helpful FAQs section, reached via the link at the bottom of the homepage, and there are loads more online resources listed on p.215 of this Rough Guide.

Basics

dkimages.com

How much will it cost?

Every feature of the MySpace site is completely free. The running of MySpace is paid for by the advertising that's plastered across the top of every page. It's possible that at some point in the future a premium service will be introduced, but for now it won't cost you a penny.

So how does MySpace work?

That's what most of this book is about, but here it is in a nutshell. When signing up as a member you are allotted your own personal "Profile" page which you use to present yourself to the world; from there you can start building up a network of friends. You get to customize your Profile in pretty much any way you want, using graphics, photos, videos and music.

Sounds rather technical?

It's not really as hard as all that. Perhaps the trickiest bit is navigating the various forms that must be edited to change the text and colours on your Profile page. From there on in you are dealing with very basic HTML code (see p.123), the same stuff that's used in every page on the World Wide Web. This code can be used to do everything from changing the colours on your page to adding images, videos and sound. This book will give you a basic grounding in code, but will also point you towards the many online resources that generate code automatically for you, so you never have to get your hands dirty.

What about pictures, sound and video? I wouldn't know where to start.

Once again, everything you need to know about preparing images, audio files and video clips for uploading to MySpace is covered in the pages of this book (see p.147 and p.157). We'll also show you how to track down and use the many freebies found all over the Web.

So what do I need to get started?

All you need is a computer with access to the Internet and an email account (see p.29). For a full walkthrough of the sign-up process, turn to p.59.

What's a MySpace friend?

It wouldn't be a network without friends. As a signed-up member of the MySpace community, you get to invite other MySpace members to become your friends and be added to your "Friends list". Once you become someone else's friend, you are also displayed on their Friends list and you get to post comments on their homepage, blog entries and picture gallery.

For more on MySpace friends, see p.83.

What else can I do on MySpace?

A surprisingly large amount. As each month goes by, more and more features are being added to the site, while everywhere else on the Web, more and more "hacks" (customizing tricks with code) are being posted for you to find and use. Just as the Internet itself has evolved over the years to become the beast it is today, so too is MySpace broadening its horizons at a staggering, and arguably unsustainable, rate.

You can do more on MySpace than we could ever cover in this book (although we'll give it our best shot), but as a taster for now, did you know that you can…

▶ **Add a top tune to your Profile page** (see p.137)

▶ **Subscribe to a blog** (see p.111)

▶ **Make your Profile private** (see p.192)

▶ **Instant message your friends** (see p.99)

▶ **Find a local gig** (see p.186)

▶ **Watch a movie trailer** (see p.118)

▶ **Play it safe** (see p.189)

Sounds good, but…

Is it going to take up a lot of my time?

Social networking is a double-edged sword. While it can be great fun to hang out and make friends on a social networking site such as MySpace, it can also become incredibly addictive. Many MySpacers find themselves spending more and more hours in front of a computer, at the expense of friends, family, work and studies. If you think you already have a problem, turn to p.204.

Do I really need a MySpace page?

Though there is pretty much something for everyone on MySpace, you certainly don't need to dive in to be part of the modern world. It's true to say that many of the individuals you come across online (just like in the real world) probably won't be your kind of people; in fact you're likely to encounter people you consider idiots at every turn. If you don't mind putting up with all this nonsense, you'll get by just fine. If, however, you are prone to being wound up by the foolishness of your fellow man, then MySpace is probably not for you.

What's all this fuss about Flash 9?

Flash is the name of the technology that MySpace uses to play back all the audio and video on the site. The music player you see on every MySpace Music Profile is a so-called "Flash widget". For any computer to be able to display these widgets, it has to have the correct version of the Adobe Flash Player installed.

In the summer of 2006, MySpace announced that they were upgrading their system to the brand new version of the software – Flash 9 –

welcome to MySpace

A brief history of MySpace

MySpace has become a huge success in little more than two years, but the story of how it all started extends back to the late 1990s, when Chris DeWolfe first met Tom Anderson at Xdrive (an online data storage company). Back then, DeWolfe, the current CEO of MySpace, ran a marketing department responsible for emailing an entertainment and technology newsletter to millions of subscribers. Anderson, now the President and "face" of MySpace, worked in the same department, analysing the newsletter's reader data and pulling together vast amounts of user information for marketing purposes. However, by 2001 Xdrive had become yet another dot-bomb, and were forced to make many of their staff redundant, including DeWolfe and Anderson's entire department.

Redeploying his knowledge of online demographics, DeWolfe almost immediately established a new company – ResponseBase – along with another email newsletter. He couldn't have done it without Anderson's help, or that of a few programmers they brought with them from Xdrive. Due to their increasingly refined ability to reach specific markets online, ResponseBase was soon purchased by eUniverse (an online marketing firm that later became Intermix Media – MySpace's parent company), and DeWolfe and Anderson used the money they made in the sale to fund the creation of MySpace.

But where did the idea for MySpace come from? At that time, social networking sites like Friendster were gaining in popularity, as were other specifically "ethnic" social sites like AsianAvenue and BlackPlanet. There were also several music networking sites on the scene, including mp3.com and MuseNet, but there was nothing that combined such seemingly disparate threads in a clean and clear fashion. The way the pages on most of these sites looked also severely limited a user's scope for interaction. MySpace changed all that. The site pushed the music edge from the very beginning and allowed its users to change their Profile page's appearance in almost any way they saw fit.

MySpace became fully operational in November 2003 and now has tens of millions of users. In 2005 Rupert Murdoch's News Corporation bought Intermix Media for a reported $580 million – mostly to get their hands on all that juicy consumer data so willingly offered by MySpace users. In a radio interview a few months after the sale, Tom Anderson remarked, "I don't have to work any more", but he's still very involved with the site – and when anyone signs up for an account, he becomes their very first "friend".

reportedly to take advantage of the various security updates included. It normally takes quite a while for Flash upgrades to be picked up by the masses, and we, "The Great Unwashed", are unlikely to even realize that an update exists until we stumble across a Flash 9 widget that requires it.

Of course, if Adobe could get one of the busiest websites in the world to jump on board, everyone else would have to follow suit quite quickly. That's what all the fuss was about. So when you are prompted to download Flash 9, just say "Yes", then you can get back to the music.

Why did MySpace sell for so much?

When MySpace was sold to News Corporation in 2005 (see box) for a figure reportedly just shy of $580 million, many commentators asked exactly the same question. But if you remember that figures circulating at the time of the sale described an online community with a population of around sixty million users, it becomes easier to understand the valuation. There's nothing advertisers like more than a massive audience; and this one came pre-wrapped with enough demographic information to keep statisticians and marketers happy for decades.

How many MySpacers are there now?

At the time of writing, the MySpace population has reportedly topped one hundred million users. However, such figures should be viewed with a little cynicism. Studies show that while MySpace generates enormous amounts of Internet traffic, perhaps as many as half the people who sign up never go back. Furthermore, only around twenty percent of registered users say that they actually visit the site more than once a week.

I thought MySpace was just something for musicians.

Almost anyone can make themselves a home on MySpace, though it's true to say that the MySpace Music community has grown to a phenomenal size at a phenomenal rate.

This is primarily because so many bands and musicians rushed to sign up

top genres	
Rock (425,660)	Pop (126,675)
Hip Hop (400,268)	Hardcore (119,104)
Rap (328,862)	Emo (101,865)
Alternative (208,639)	Electronica (95,117)
R&B (196,764)	Techno (54,470)
Experimental (192,402)	Death Metal (53,325)
Other (187,394)	Christian (50,374)
Indie (180,214)	Folk (50,102)
Acoustic (171,233)	Electro (49,149)
Metal (159,982)	Pop Punk (48,484)
Punk (148,501)	Progressive (47,379)

Next »

in the early days of the site (see box, p.54). They were quickly partitioned off into their own area with their own specific Profile features. To get an idea of just how much music is up there, take a look at the "Top Genres" box on the Music homepage (music. myspace.com). Where else on the planet could you find over 400,000 hip-hop acts rubbing shoulders with 50,000 death met-allers and an equal number of Christian rockers?

Is it safe?

The world is a dangerous place and just like everything else, MySpace has its own specific dangers (which you have no doubt read about in great detail in the media). The biggest danger is ignorance – on the part of both MySpacers and those looking in from the outside. So to get all the information and advice you need to use MySpace safely, turn to p.191. For the answers to more general common concerns about safety, security and privacy within online communities, turn back to the previous chapter (p.37).

I don't understand a word of it.

Just as the now-accepted art of mobile phone texting spawned its own language of abbreviations, slang and acronyms, so

MySpace has also created its own vocabulary. A mixture of hip-hop speak, mall chat, text blather and playground banter has evolved, and it is being documented online, every day.

The basics are fairly easy to pick up. "The" translates as "da", and if you want to ask something nicely, you say "pleze", etc. You can also expect to come across loads of text wRItTeN SoMeTHinG LikE thIS! For some more advanced vocabulary, check out one of the many online slang dictionaries, and you'll soon know the difference between "MySpace jackin'" and "MySpace hopping" – and perhaps learn how to get your "MySpace angles" just right.

Slang Dictionary www.urbandictionary.com
The Source www.thesource4ym.com/teenlingo

If you want to have a go at making up your own slang, try:

The Infinite Teen Slang Dictionary thesurrealist.co.uk/slang

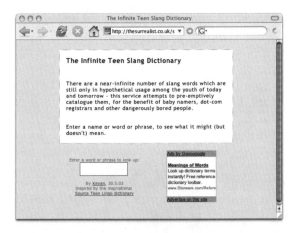

06
Your first time

getting started

G iven that most people who sign up to MySpace are doing so to hook up with a gaggle of friends already online, you probably have a fairly good idea of what to expect from your first session. And if you are an average Internet-savvy teenager, you may feel that you can skip this section of the book altogether. That said, some of the information you provide and the choices you make when first signing up are worth considering carefully, and there may well be a few things you haven't yet considered lurking in the following pages.

Creating an account

As we just stated, some of these instructions are going to be very basic, but they are still worth glancing at. This chapter is written with MySpace in mind, but almost everything covered here will be relevant, or at least similar, to other online community sites.

With MySpace, assuming you haven't been invited to sign up by a friend sending an email (see p.85), the first thing you need to do is navigate to the MySpace website.

The address, as you might expect, is www.myspace.com. Thanks to a few clever Internet tricks, you should immediately end up staring at the homepage of your "local" MySpace site: check for a

Make room for your folks

Just as parents are rarely to be seen "hanging out" in playgrounds and shopping malls, part of the attraction of MySpace and other social networking sites for many teenagers is the fact that they represent an adult-free environment. These sites offer a place where teens can talk candidly to their friends and experiment with their images and means of expression. This rite of passage is something that all parents have themselves gone through, albeit in very different arenas. As such, before parents can ever hope to be able to talk to their kids about what they get up to online, they need to understand the language and structure of these sites.

By far the best way to do this is by signing up themselves. We are in no way condoning parents gate-crashing their offspring's circle of friends. That's about as uncool as it gets. Instead, parents need to come to grips with how it all works and then perhaps join one of the many parenting rings that can be found in the "Family & Home" MySpace groups directory (see p.104).

little flag on the blue title strip at the top of the page that relates to the region: UK, US, Ireland, France, etc. If you don't end up at the regional page you were after, click the "International" link on the right and navigate from there.

It's worth noting that www.myspace.com is the only sure-fire way to get to MySpace. www.myspace.co.uk, for example, does not take you to MySpace, even though the page you stumble upon seems to offer MySpace-style social networking services.

Once you've found the site, you could just decide to start browsing (see p.82) or searching (see p.79) for your buddies and

The MySpace homepage in all its glory – the place to start, whether you're browsing, searching or setting up a new account.

other interesting people. However, you'll soon discover that you aren't going to make any friends like that, and you certainly aren't going to be able to communicate with anyone without your own account. It's time to sign up.

The sign-up process

To begin the account set-up process, simply click the "SignUp" button in the top-right corner of the page and fill out the online form that appears.

The form is pretty self-explanatory and you will need to fill in all the information before it will allow you to move on. With regard to privacy, don't worry for now – you get to choose exactly how much of your personal information is made public later on. By default, your Profile page will only publicly display your first name, age and location. Over the following pages are a few more tips to get you through this first page.

Tip: When signing up as a musician or filmmaker the process is almost the same, but you will need to start via the respective SignUp links on the MySpace Music and Film homepages.

VERY IMPORTANT!!!

You have to be 14 YEARS OLD to sign up for a MySpace account. MySpace have cracked down on underage account holders, and many have had their accounts deleted. You have been warned.

Email address

Many people these days have several different email accounts, and when signing up with an online community such as MySpace, it is well worth having an email address that you use exclusively for that purpose. Once you get started, the "Friends Requests" and "Message Alerts" will start coming thick and fast, which can be very distracting when they're jumbled in with every-day work, college or school emails. There is also the problem of the spam emails that come hand-in-hand with a social networking account. Equally, you may discover that your office, school or college will not look favourably upon you using "their" email address on a social networking site.

Passwords

Your MySpace password has to be at least six characters long and contain both letters and either digits or punctuation marks. This makes it much harder for identity thieves to second-guess passwords. MySpace will not allow you to create a password that too

Tip: If you ever suspect that your password has become public, change it immediately via the "Account Settings" link on your Hello page. You should also consider changing your password every month or so as a matter of course.

closely resembles your name (for example, if you are lucky enough to be called Peter, don't even bother trying to use "PETER1" as your password). Equally, don't create a password that might be guessed by your peers or family – favourite bands, pets, and girl-friends' and boyfriends' names, etc, should all be avoided.

Verification

Copying the psychedelic lettering from the graphic you are shown into the verification text field is a necessary feature that ensures the new account is not being created by a "bot" (an auto-mated form-filling program). If you get it wrong the first time you try, MySpace will give you another crack at it.

Terms of Service

You have to check the box that indicates you have read the MySpace "Terms of Service" and "Privacy Policy". These are important documents and it is well worth knowing exactly what you are agreeing to when you sign up. If you do break any of the rules and are reported (see p.205), you run the serious risk of having your account deleted.

> **Tip for parents:** Be sure that you understand the rules that govern MySpace – it will undoubtedly aid any discussions you have with your children on the subject. You can refer to them at any time by clicking the "Terms" link at the bottom of the MySpace homepage.

Uploading your first picture

Once you get through the first form and hit "Sign Up", you are then prompted to upload your first image, which will (until you

> **Tip:** If you don't have a photo you like, or really don't know where to start, click the "Skip for now" button and come back to it later after reading this book's image primer on p.147.

change it) be your face on MySpace. Again, it is worth taking a moment to read the MySpace "Picture Policy", but, in a nutshell, it says you shouldn't submit anything offensive or rude, or the copyrighted work of others.

MySpace does not automatically resize or re-format your images for the Web when you upload them, so they need to be right before you start. You are only permitted to submit photos saved in either the JPG or GIF file format, and each file must be smaller than 600k in file size.

> **Tip:** Think carefully about the images you upload to MySpace. What do you want them to say about you? In terms of your own privacy, be sure that they don't give away anything you wouldn't want to be within the public domain – does the photo show you standing next to the sign of the street where you live? Are you wearing that scarf knitted by Auntie Jane that has your mobile phone number stitched around the trim? You get the idea.

This is all explained in far more detail on p.149, along with image tips and pointers to free photo-editing tools that should help.

Your image should upload in a matter of seconds, but don't be

welcome to MySpace

surprised if it takes a few attempts and error messages to get your first image up. You will soon discover that MySpace can be a little temperamental at times, and you will often encounter discouraging failure and error messages (see p.203).

With your first image uploaded, you will find yourself gazing

Tip: It's important to realize that there *is* a difference between your personal MySpace Hello page (where you maintain the various features of your account) and your MySpace "Profile" page, which the rest of the world gets to look at. You alone may view the former when logged into MySpace, while the latter can be reached by anyone via your unique MySpace URL (see below).

at your very own MySpace "Home" page – which from this point on will be refered to as the "Hello page".

Choose your MySpace Name/URL

This is very important and should be sorted out a.s.a.p. Your URL (an acronym for the rather unfriendly sounding term

---

Help

Pick your MySpace Name/URL!
Click Here

Tell people about your MySpace [?]

My URL
http://www.myspace.com/104035005

My Blog URL
http://blog.myspace.com/104035005

Uniform Resource Locator) is simply your page's address on the World Wide Web – the thing that people will have to type into their Web browser to visit your Profile.

Looking at your newly forged Hello page, you will notice that MySpace has already assigned you a shiny new URL that begins,

Tip: If you find that your name has already been used by someone else (eg, www.myspace.com/johnsmith), try introducing an underscore character (eg, www.myspace.com/john_smith) when MySpace asks you to have another stab.

as you might expect, http://www.myspace.com/, but ends with a string of numbers – not very catchy. MySpace refers to this URL-ending as your "MySpace Name" which, confusingly, is not the same thing as your "Display Name" (see p.71) – the name that everyone sees at the top of your Profile page.

Tip for parents: Talk to your kids about how they choose their MySpace Names and Display Names. Compromise, from both parties, may sometimes be required when what they see as "cool" you understand to be provocative or offensive.

To define your MySpace Name and URL, click the link and enter your desired moniker. It can be anything you want, not necessarily your real name, and it must be unique – no two web-pages can have the same address. Also be aware that it cannot contain any spaces and nearly all punctuation marks and special characters (see tip above) are also out of play. You only get one chance at this and then it's set in stone, so think carefully and get a friend to look over your shoulder to check for typos.

Edit your Profile

You don't have to add any more information to your Profile than the basic information you've already added, but most people do. It's worth remembering that the more details and personality

Previewing your Profile

When you are logged into MySpace, to preview your Profile page from your Hello page (where you maintain and change your account details, etc) click the "Profile" link below your default image.

To return to your account's Hello page, click the "Home" link on the far left of the MySpace navigation bar.

The "Home" link can be used to reach your Hello page from any MySpace page when you are logged in.

69

> **Tip:** If you want the main MySpace homepage to open every time you start your Web browser (see p.32), click the "Make MySpace my Home Page" link on your Hello page. If you'd rather be greeted each time with your own Profile page, highlight the URL in the "Tell people about your MySpace" box on your Hello page, and then drag it onto the little house icon on your browser's toolbar.

your page displays, the easier it is for individuals viewing your Profile to build an image of who you are … perhaps a true image, perhaps not. There's nothing wrong with experimenting with your persona – everybody does in the various facets of their lives – but try to think about how someone else will relate to you when all they have to go on is a single page. Equally, think about what those who *do* know you will make of your online personality.

To get started, select the "Edit Profile" option found in the list next to your image at the top of your Hello page. This takes you to the "Profile Edit" page. Clicking through the page's tabs reveals numerous sets of fields where you can add your personal details. The key here is to balance your privacy against your "searchability". The more information you provide, the easier it is for people to make connections to you – that's what social networking is all about. But your privacy is also very important, and there are enough bad apples out there to make it worth thinking long and

> **Tip:** Though you can dive straight in with HTML (see p.124) to change the way your "Interests & Personality" information looks on your Profile page, it's probably best to just get the words right for now and worry about the rest later.

> **Tip:** Don't feel you have to compose your blurbs and lists in those pokey little online fields. Longer diatribes are always best tackled offline in a dedicated text application such as Microsoft Word – especially if you pay for Internet access by the minute or might benefit from a "spell checker". When your text is written and ready to go, simply copy it (using the keyboard shortcuts Ctrl+C or Apple+C) from your text editor and paste it (Ctrl+V or Apple+V) into the appropriate "Profile Edit" field.

hard about how you want to play it. Here's a quick run through the profile cues that need a little additional comment.

Interests & Personality

The most important field of the form is "About Me". It can be as long or as short as you want, and it can be written in whatever style you desire – tell the world who you are. It's worth reading a few other people's efforts before you start, to get an idea of what kinds of things you might say. Remember, first impressions matter.

Name

If you do nothing else, be sure to take a look under the "Name" tab; this is where you get to set your "Display Name", which everyone will see when they view your Profile page. This is best kept short and sweet as it will appear above your thumbnail image in Friends lists (see p.78), bulletin

> **Tip for parents:** For a little extra MySpace anonymity, you could encourage your kids to delete their first and last names, only leaving their Display Name intact. This will make them harder to track down via the MySpace search functions.

posts (see p.109) and messages (see p.92). If it's any longer than eleven or twelve characters it will get chopped midway on "View All Friends" pages.

Basic Information/Background & Lifestyle

Nothing under these tabs needs attention other than your gender, country, date of birth and marital status. As for the rest, if there are things you would rather people didn't know about you, just leave the fields blank or select "No answer" from the dropdown menus.

Schools/Companies

For many teenagers, MySpace represents an important extension of day-to-day school life, so entering these details seems an obvi-

Special characters

Though it is easy enough to fill in all this text-based information without worrying about HTML code (which we will come to later, see p.123), you may find that you want to use certain so-called "special characters" or foreign language characters that either are not present on your keyboard or don't display properly when you preview your text. These characters need to be replaced by special "name codes". For example, the Trademark™ character is represented by ™ while an uppercase É (with an acute accent) has the name code É. For a full list of special character name codes, visit: www.xgenerators.com/index.php?x=specialcharacters

ous thing to do. It does, however, represent a significant source of information for anyone wanting to track down a MySpacer in the real world.

Entering information about present or past employment can also make it easy for people to deduce where you might live, so think hard about whether you think this information will really add anything to your MySpace experience.

Networking

Selecting areas of interests from the dropdown menu under this tab is, again, a means of making yourself more accessible to the wider MySpace community. To see what it means for your "searchability", turn to p.77.

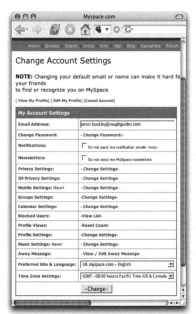

Change Account Settings

Accessed from the list next to the photo on your Hello page, the "Change Account Settings" form is a very useful tool that's worth familiarizing yourself with.

This is where you come to do everything from changing your password to tweaking your Profile's music settings (see p.137), and perhaps most importantly, adjusting your privacy settings. You can explore all these options yourself as they are relatively self-explanatory, though to read the full story on "Privacy Settings" and hiding your identity, turn to p.192.

Logging out and logging in

Before going any further it is essential that you understand the importance of logging out at the end of your MySpace sessions. Closing your browser window or even quitting your browser does not mean that you have logged out of MySpace – anyone coming to the same computer and viewing MySpace may well find themselves logged in as you, with full access to your account. This is, of course, of particular concern if you are using computers in public places, such as libraries, schools or Internet cafés. Equally, if more than one person in your household has a MySpace account, you could quite easily find yourself accidentally logged in and making Friends Requests, etc, under someone else's name.

So here is the golden rule: at the end of every session, click the "SignOut" link that can be found at the top of every MySpace page, just above the advertising banner.

Tip: To check, at any time, whether or not you are logged in, hit the "Home" link on the far left of the main MySpace navigation strip. If you are logged in, the link will take you to your "Hello" page; if you're not, it will load the MySpace homepage.

To log back in again, find your way to the MySpace homepage and use the "Member Login" box to enter your email address and password.

Finally, as a precaution, never check any boxes offering to "remember" your login details, either on a MySpace page or on a browser dialog box.

Tip: If you're spending time away in the wilderness, or do not intend to log in for a while, you can set MySpace to send the equivalent of an out-of-office message to anyone who tries tp contact you. Click "View / Edit Away Message" at the bottom of the "Account Settings" page and enter your note in the screen that appears.

How to delete your account

If you make a complete hash of your first session, don't be afraid to delete your new account and start all over again. Though most of the information you have added will be editable, it is often easier to start from scratch. Be aware, however, that you may not be able to reuse the email address from a deleted account if you create a new account straight away – the old address should be available to use again after around 48 hours.

If it's your new MySpace URL you have a problem with (which isn't editable), then deleting your account is the only way to wipe the slate clean. Before you proceed, make sure you have back-up copies of all your photos, blog entries, etc stored somewhere else, as any already uploaded content will be deleted along with your account. Here's how it's done:

▶ From your Hello page click "Account Settings" (it's at the top, just next to your default photo).

▶ Next click the small red text that reads "cancel account". Read the on-screen warnings, and click the red button that reads "Cancel My Account".

▶ You are then prompted to offer a reason for your departure – this is not mandatory, so just hit this page's red button to continue.

▶ MySpace then emails you a link (thus ensuring that the true account holder has requested the deletion) which takes you to a page where you are asked one final time whether you want to continue…

▶ From this point it should take no more than a couple of days for your old profile to vanish from the MySpace system.

07

Searching & browsing

where to start

N ow that you are up and running, it's time to broaden your horizons, put some feelers out and get a better idea of what MySpace has to offer. In this chapter you'll learn just how easy it is to find old friends and search for new ones.

Web | **MySpace** | People | Music | Blogs | Video ▶

Search MySpace

Friends

For those not already in the know, MySpace is primarily about managing your list of friends. If you look at any Profile page on MySpace, you'll see an area (normally on the right) reserved for friends' thumbnails. This area will also include a link to view all of a user's friends (pictured below). Many teenagers simply use the site as a means of staying in contact with a small circle of real-world peers, but others hop around the network, via the thumbnail links, accumulating a Friends list with a roll call of thousands. This activity is often called MySpace "whoring". Of course, most of the these accumulated "friends" are barely even online acquaintances, they are just numbers in a highly competitive game of "who's-got-the-most-pals".

The "View All Friends" page. By default MySpace lets the world know when you are online; to disable this function, see p.195.

Tip for parents: Accumulating "friends" simply for the sake of it is not to be encouraged, and does little more than increase an individual's online visibility in an uncontrollable way.

Find people

So, you know that you can seek people out by "hopping" from Friends lists to new Profile pages. And if you are looking for someone in your immediate circle of real-world friends, this might be all you need to do. You could also try second-guessing their MySpace URL and finding them that way. However, these are not the only ways to search for people on MySpace. Below are descriptions of a few more of the tools at your disposal.

Search tools

The Search box at the top of most MySpace pages is easy to use, though give its "Web search" option a wide berth – the results are

Six degrees of separation

Everyone, now and again, finds themselves chatting to a stranger who happens to know someone, who knows someone, who knows them… "It's a small world", you might hear yourself say. But just how small is it? For decades scientists have been trying to quantify the "global network", most famously resulting in the notion of "six degrees of separation". The phrase first appeared in the late 1960s when a study by psychologist Stanley Milgram concluded that any two random US citizens were, at any given time, connected by a chain of, at most, six acquaintances. These kinds of studies continue to this day, and even with the added arena of the Internet factored into the equation, researchers are still coming up with figures of between five and seven degrees of separation. But what about MySpace? Perhaps we need to prepare ourselves for a world with only two degrees of separation … where everyone knows Tom!

> **Tip:** In Firefox (see p.33), use the "tabbed browsing" feature to open multiple friends pages simultaneously. You might want to check the "Disable Band Songs From Automatically Starting" box under "Privacy Settings", however, when viewing several Profiles that all stream music!

not as exact as those you might get from Google.

On Profile pages, the search box has only two options – search "MySpace" or search "The Web". To get the more complex version of the search box, hit "Home" on the main navigation strip. From there you can specify whether you are simply looking for "People", or if you want to search within one of the main MySpace communities for particular "Music", "Blogs" or "Video".

For even more search fields, click "Search" on the main MySpace navigation bar. This page of search parameters (see below) ties in

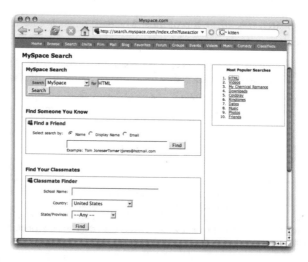

Tip: If you don't want people to be able to find you using the MySpace Search tools, don't add the relevant information to your Profile page (see p.71).

with some of the information that users choose to add to their Profile (see p.71). More specifically, this page can be used to find people by name, email address, schools attended (see below) or networking activities (see p.73).

Look up your school friends

You can find school friends, either current or long-lost, using the "Find Your Classmates" section of the "MySpace Search" page (described above) or from the "Schools" homepage. To reach the "Schools" homepage, click on the link in the tinted box below the main navigation strip on the MySpace homepage. It can also be reached using the URL schools.myspace.com.

Once you find a match for your school's name, you are given lots of options for fine-tuning your search – you can search by everything from academic department to year of graduation.

You also have the option of tracking down friends via your school's "Groups" (see p.103). Click the "Groups" link on the main MySpace navigation bar, and either browse the "Schools & Alumni" category or go straight to the "Search Groups" link on the left. From there, you can type in the school's name and then refine your search using the various options in the dropdown menu on the right.

Though it's a long shot, you might also try your luck in MySpace Forums (see p.106). Click the "Forums" link on the MySpace navigation bar, and then browse the "Campus Life" category.

> **Tip:** Apple OS X Tiger users can add a MySpace search widget to their Dashboard. Download it from:
> apple.com/downloads/dashboard/search/myspacesearch.html

Browse

Also found via a link on the main MySpace navigation bar, the "Browse" form offers another way to dive into the MySpace community, though it offers you little hope of finding a specific person as its search criteria are very general. It's much better suited to finding random people with interests or a lifestyle similar to your own. Use either the "Basic" or "Advanced" views to get started.

> **Tip for parents:** If you are worried about your child's visibility on MySpace, sit down at the computer with them and check just how easy it is to find them using the various tools and specific search criteria. For more on privacy, see p.192.

08
Making friends

breaking the ice

Now that you know how to search for people and track down old acquaintances and school chums on MySpace, it's time to start populating your list of friends. Although a quick look at MySpace might lead you to believe that this process is a complete free-for-all, it is in fact a two-step process, involving one person asking to become friends and another person allowing it. This chapter takes a look at the basics of making friends within MySpace, as well as the things you can do to safeguard the process.

Fill your list

The way you use your Friends list will largely determine the kind of MySpacer you are. At one end of the spectrum, a small group of friends might each maintain a small list, containing only each other's names. At the other extreme, some MySpacers make it their goal to inch their way up the MySpace charts by collecting friends like there's no tomorrow, even going so far as to get others to "whore" (see p.89) their Profile in an attempt to get as many "adds" (additions to other people's lists) as possible.

Even if you don't go that far, it feels good to have a healthy, growing Friends list. However, it's not just about the numbers – it can also be about *who* you know. Many MySpacers have at least a few celebrity names in their list, more often than not as a means of showing the kind of person *they* are – the music and movies *they* like – rather than any real attempt to become best buddies with Madonna or Eminem.

> **Tip:** If you are signed up as a MySpace Artist (see p.169), your Friends list is a fantastic way to boost your profile and get yourself heard – by potential fans, collaborators, record labels and your own musical heroes.

What's more, your friends don't have to be individuals. Though you probably already know that you can send friend requests to bands, it's also open season for films, record labels and even inanimate objects. Fancy making friends with a Starbucks Frappuccino (www.myspace.com/starbuxfrapp) or a 60 gig iPod (www.myspace.com/60gbipod)?

Additionally, having "friends" within MySpace allows you certain privileges. Bulletins (see p.109), for example, can only be sent to people on your Friends list.

Invite friends

If you are one of the first of your peers to get into MySpace, go ahead and invite your friends to join up too. Click the "Invite" link on the main MySpace navigation strip. From there you can either add email addresses to your invite manually or (if you have an AOL, Gmail, Hotmail or Yahoo! email account) import whole lists of contacts in one fell swoop. You can add a message to your invite as well as a personalized invite link that will automatically add new users to your Friends list when they sign up. To reveal your link, click "show my invite link".

Tip: Many social networking sites, such as the Google-owned orkut, are run on a purely "invitation only" basis. To find out more, turn to p.21.

Request a friend

Making friends in this way is, as you might expect, very straightforward. Find the Profile page of the person you want to add to your list and click the "Add to Friends" link in their "Contacting…" box. You will then be asked to confirm the request (see below), and your potential pal will then receive a "New Friend Request Message".

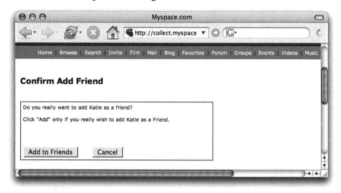

Accept or deny

Let's turn the tables for a moment and assume it's you receiving the "New Friend Request Message". This message will come to you as an email (see tip below) and will also appear in a special MySpace Friends Requests inbox. On your Hello page, look out for "New Friend Requests!" alerts in the top of your "My Mail" box

Tip: If you do not want to receive "Friend Request" alerts via email, disable the feature via the "Account Settings" page, which is reached using the link on your Hello page.

(see right). You don't have to deal with a request right away; pending requests will sit in your inbox for a month. Once you've clicked the link, you are taken to the "Friends Request Manager" page.

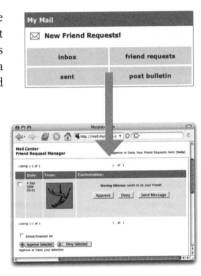

Many MySpacers, at this point, throw caution to the wind and blindly accept every request that comes their way. You can even download software that will do it for you. This is, however, not good karma. If you want to have a meaningful "network" of friends, rather than an online butterfly collection that might harbour the odd psycho, be selective about whose requests you accept (and don't worry about upsetting anyone, no message is sent to say that you have declined a Friend Request). Also, don't be afraid to send a message to any unknown "requester" to find out exactly what they're about and why they've chosen to contact you. At the very least, take a look at their Profile page before agreeing to give them an "add".

Tip: When you do get accepted onto someone's Friends list, it's nice to say "thanks for the add" in a comment (see p.95). First up, it's a good way to break the ice, and secondly, it lets others viewing their page know that you are new to the block.

87

If you are dealing with several requests at one time, use the check boxes to the left of the page and the "Approve Selected" and "Deny Selected" buttons at the bottom to speed through the process.

> **Tip for parents:** Encourage your kids, especially the younger ones, to limit their friends to people they know in the real world. When they do want to broaden their horizons, be sure they understand the dangers of fake Profiles (see p.38).

Get verification

If you want to limit the ease with which other people can add you to their Friends list, look under "Account Settings" for the "Privacy Settings" link. Check the box labelled "Require email or last name to add me as a friend". From that point on, potential friends will have to know either your surname or your email address to send you a Friend Request – in short, they need to know you

ouside of MySpace to become your friend. Of course, if your surname is part of your "Display Name" (see p.71), everyone will know what it is anyway – so make sure it isn't.

MySpace whoring

"Whoring" on MySpace has come to mean several different things, but is most widely used to describe the act of trying to "big up" either your own or someone else's Profile to garner a ton of "adds". This process normally involves posting picture comments (see p.98) on other people's Profiles, that do little more than shout "ADD ME", "ADD HIM" or "ADD HER". There are loads of sites online that will generate link codes so that when people click on them they automatically send a Friend Request to the person you are "bigging up". There are better ways to spend your time online.

Manage your list

When you first sign up with MySpace, your Friends list has only one occupant: Tom. Once your list starts to fill, you will notice that only a handful of your Friends are displayed on your main Profile page and Hello page. These are your "Top Friends". By default, only four appear at any one time, but you can re-order them, rotate them and increase the number that are visible (see below).

To view your entire list of friends, click the "View All..." links in the "Friends" area of either your Hello page or Profile page.

Change your "Top Friends"

At the bottom of the "Friends" area of your Hello page click

89

> **Tip:** If you want to display even more of your friends on your Profile page, or customize the way your Friends list is displayed, search online for a special code generator. This one is pretty good: www.rapidcodes.com/friends

"Change My Top Friends". You will be taken to a page where you can change the number of displayed friends (at the time of writing the dropdown menu offers a maximum of 24) and, by dragging and dropping the thumbnails, change your selected "Top Friends". Rather than having to scroll through page after page of friends to find a specific thumbnail to add to the top table, use the "Friend Finder Filter" box. You can also drag and drop the thumbnails to change the order in which your Top Friends are displayed. It's all very easy.

Remove friends

You can delete friends from your Friends list at any time. Log in to MySpace and go to your Hello page. Click the "Edit Friends" link in the "Friends" section of the page. Check the box next to the friend you want to get rid of, and then click "Delete Selected" at the bottom of the page.

Don't worry about upsetting them – no message is sent to inform them that they have been removed from your Friends list.

09

Mail, comments & chat

It's good to talk

MySpace is about a lot more than just your list of friends; it's about communicating, expressing yourself and being part of something dynamic and exciting. This chapter looks at the numerous communication tools you have at your disposal as a member of MySpace, and briefly shows you how to use them efficiently and safely.

Mail

Unlike regular email, MySpace Mail does not allow you to send messages over the wider Internet, but only within the MySpace community. By default, however, you will be sent an email (to the

address you use to log in) every time you receive a message via MySpace Mail – you don't get the actual message, just an alert.

To view messages you have received, log in to MySpace and head to your "Mail Center Inbox" by either clicking the "Mail" link on the main MySpace navigation bar or clicking the "Inbox" link on your "Hello" page. From there, viewing and reading your messages is completely self-explanatory, so there's no reason to waste your time discussing it here.

Tip: If you do not want to receive MySpace Mail alerts in your regular email account (the one you use to log in to MySpace), disable the feature via the "Account Settings" page, which is reached using the link on your Hello page. Simply check the box that reads "Do not send me notification emails".

Tip: If you start receiving "spam", "junk" emails, or offensive emails in your MySpace Mail inbox, click the "spam/abuse Flag" link to the right of the message. It will disappear from your inbox and the MySpace authorities will investigate its source.

Send messages

To send a message to another MySpacer using MySpace Mail, you have several options:

▶ **Reply** Every Mail message that you receive has a "Reply" button at the bottom – easy!

▶ **Send Message** To send any MySpace user a Mail message, find their Profile page and hit the "Send Message" link.

▶ **Address Book** From your MySpace Address Book (see overleaf), click the red envelope icon that appears in the MySpace Profile column. This is only available if the person has a valid MySpace "UserName".

Once you've clicked the "Send" button, a copy of your message is filed away in your "Sent" folder. There's a link to it in the panel on the left of all Mail-related pages; this panel also features various

> **Tip:** To use MySpace Mail to tell someone from your Friends list about a particular Profile page, click the "Forward to Friend" link on the Profile page you want to shout about and then choose a message recipient from the dropdown menu.

> **Tip:** You can also get MySpace "Mobile Alerts" sent to your mobile phone in the form of text messages, though your network may charge you for the privilege. To set things up, click the "Mobile Settings" link on your "Account Settings" page.

other shortcuts and links that you should find useful. Messages sit in your Sent folder for fourteen days and are then automatically deleted, so if you compose something particularly witty that you want to keep, copy and paste the text somewhere else – you could even stick it in a blog (see p.111) for the world to see.

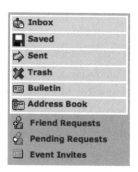

Your Address Book

To view your MySpace Address Book, log in and click the "Manage Address Book" link just to the right of your picture on your Hello page.

There are two ways to add individuals to your Address Book; either use the "Quick Add Contact" form at the bottom of the page, or hit the "Add a Contact" link on the left, which offers a fuller set of contact information fields for you to fill in. If you ever need to go back and edit any of this information, click the "Edit" link on the far right of an entry's line in the main Address Book view. On the left, you will also notice a link to the "Lists" function, which can be used to group different sets of individual entries together.

Though it is useful to know that MySpace has this contacts tool, at the time of writing the Address Book functionality is not really good enough to replace whatever other contact management software you might use. And with regard to MySpace usability, it is far easier to go straight to a Friend's Profile page via your Friends list and Mail them using the link there.

The MySpace Address Book's one redeeming feature is that all your contact details are accessible wherever you are – though this in turn raises the danger that someone could easily access all that data if you ever failed to log off a public computer (see p.28).

Comments

Comments are one of the most important means of communication on MySpace; more than just an email message, they are public notes, posted on Profile pages for all to see. They can also be added to the "View My Pics" page and blog entries.

Adding comments is very easy. Make sure you are logged in and keep an eye out for the "Add Comment" links on Profile pages, blogs and photo pages. You have

to be a user's friend to post a comment on one of their pages, though, by default, it's open season on blogs (see p.111).

The most common, and most public, place that you'll come across comments is on Profile pages. Comments can do everything from just saying hello, to congratulating a band on their music, or offering an invitation to a party or gig. When your friends post new comments to your page you will receive an email alert and a message in the "Mail" area of your Hello page.

But let's not be naive about this: comments are not always "nice". Comments turning up on Profile pages can sometimes be offensive, embarrassing or humiliating, or they may just be junk. Whatever the reason, you will, on occasion, want to remove comments from your Profile page, or perhaps even stop them from appearing in the first place. Here are the basics:

Manage your comments

▶ **To block comments that contain HTML** check "Disable HTML Comments" under "Account Settings". This will stop people posting comments on your Profile page that contain images, video, flash files, etc.

▶ **To only let friends comment on your blog** check the appropriate button on your "Privacy Settings" page.

> **Tip for parents:** If your kids insist on allowing others to post comments on their pages – and they probably will – encourage them to check for new comments regularly, or even set their account so that they have to approve each comment before it's posted (see opposite).

Safe Edit Mode

HTML codes can be added to comments to insert images, videos or whatever. If someone posts some bad code in a comment on your page and all that's displayed on your profile page is either jumbled text or a broken link icon, you can use "Safe Edit Mode" to go in and deal with the offending code. From the "Profile Edit" page click the link in the top-right corner and then select the "Comments" tab.

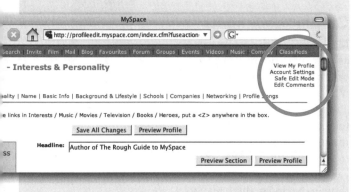

▶ **To delete a Profile comment** either hit the "New Comment" link when it appears on your Hello page and look for the "Delete" link next to the offending comment, or click "Edit Profile" at the top of your Hello page and then the "Edit Comments" link on the right.

▶ **To approve comments before they are posted** click "Account Settings" on your Hello page, and then click the red link next to "Privacy Settings" and check the appropriate button. From now on you will receive an email alert whenever a new comment is posted.

▶ **To delete a picture comment** click the "Pics" link below the default photo on your Hello page. Click the image that contains the offending comment and hit "delete".

Graphic comments

Many MySpacers post images as part of a comment, which can be a very eye-catching way to get yourself noticed. Take a look around MySpace to get an idea of the kind of things people post.

Though to the uninitiated it can seem like a rather "techie" thing to be doing, there really is no secret expertise required. All you need to do is host your image somewhere online (see p.154) and then paste an HTML link to its location in the text field when you compose your comment. Something like this will do the job:

My message here
<img src="http://www.myserver.com/myimage.jpg">

> **Tip:** Video comments work in basically the same way as image comments. For more on creating video for MySpace, see p.157, or point your browser at: foureyedmonsters.com/tutorial

Chat

Chat, also known as
"Instant Messaging"
or IM (and not to be
confused with "chat
rooms", see p.101),
is another very use-
ful way to commu-
nicate with friends
on MySpace. IM
involves connecting

My IM Privacy Settings

○	No one can IM me.
◉	Only Friends can IM me.
○	Anyone can IM me.

Change Settings **Cancel**

with other MySpacers and typing real-time messages to each
other – a little like a text-based telephone conversation.

The main hurdle to overcome when getting started is that
by default all MySpace accounts are set not to allow Instant
Messaging. You will need to go into your "Account Settings" and
enable the function in the options reached by clicking the "IM
Privacy Settings" link. It is not recommended that you check the
button that reads "Anyone can IM me", because that's just asking
for trouble; it's best to keep it between you and your friends (if
you have thousands of friends in your list it's probably best to
leave the function disabled).

The next thing to do is to make sure that anyone you want to
IM makes the same changes to their "IM Privacy Settings" as
you've just made.

Make contact

Once you and your friends are set up, log in and go to a friend's
Profile page – they don't have to be online for you to send them a

message, but obviously they do if you want to get a reply straight away. In their "Contacting…" area, click the "Instant Message" link and wait to be connected. Once your IM window opens, type your text into the long strip near the bottom, using the various buttons to style what you've written and add "smilies" if you wish. Hit "send" when you're done, and away you go…

MySpaceIM

At the time of writing, MySpace are on the point of introducing a brand new Instant Messenger application for MySpacers. It will have far more features than the system described above, but it will initially only be available to Windows PC users. For full details, visit: www.myspace.com/myspaceim

Chat rooms

MySpace chat rooms work a little like a communal version of IM Chat and are sporadically policed by "chat moderators". These rooms can be great fun to use and are very popular, though it can take a while to grasp the thread of what is going on – you will often find yourself staring at the computer screen, watching the banter rack up, but with no real idea how to interject.

To kick off, choose which of the many chat rooms on MySpace you want to plug in to. On the MySpace homepage, click the "Chat Rooms" link in the panel below the main navigation bar.

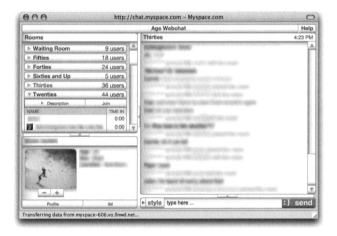

Tip: If you want to home in on any one member of the chat room and send them an instant message, select their image in the panel on the left and click the "IM" button at the bottom.

> **Tip for parents:** Though they'll probably make a bee-line for them anyway, teenagers should be encouraged to browse the "Age" section of the chat room listings for the teens-only rooms, which are out-of-bounds to anyone with a stated age of above twenty. Of course, there is nothing to stop adults with Profiles that misrepresent their age from entering chat rooms, so make sure your kids are aware of this fact.

From there, you can browse lists by category, global location or age. Click one you fancy trying out, and dive in.

The interface is similar to that of IM and you'll soon get the idea of how it works. It's always polite to announce your presence with something chirpy such as "Hi folks!", and you should at least try to grasp the basics of online chat etiquette and vocabulary. For a quick primer, point your Web browser at:
www.goodchatting.com/articles/etiquette.phtml

When you've had enough, say goodbye to whoever you're talking to and leave the chat room by closing the open frame. In Windows use the button in the top-right corner; in Mac OS X it can be found top-left.

10

Groups &
forums

something for everyone

This chapter introduces the various groups and forums that exist beneath the MySpace umbrella. They offer a way to share your experiences and knowledge with other MySpacers who have interests similar to yours. Groups are the more formal entity, in that you have to join one to take part. Forums, on the other hand, are more informal and any MySpacer can post a comment or add to the debate at any time. Compared to regular MySpace life, the etiquette of these arenas is very precise – time-wasters and attention-seekers are rarely tolerated.

MySpace Groups

Groups might be relatively regimented in structure, but they are still diverse and wacky in terms of content – only on MySpace could a group called "I Sing and Dance in My Car when Everyone Is Looking" have over ten thousand members.

Each group has a moderator or group leader, and depending on how conscientious the moderators are, groups can be either very useful entities or a general scrum of spam and junk posts.

To track down and join an existing group, hit the "Groups" link on the main MySpace navigation bar and then either browse the numerous categories or search for a group by keyword. From there a couple of links will get you signed up with any one specific group. Explore the various options offered on each group page

– there are photos pages, an "Invite" tool, a link to start new topics in the forums section (also called the "Message Board") of the group, etc. It's also worth taking a minute to look at your "Privacy" settings for the groups you are a member of: click the link in the panel next to your Group Leader's image.

> **Tip:** To quickly find a group that you have previously joined, click "Groups" on the MySpace navigation bar, and then "My Groups" in the blue panel on the left.

> **Tip:** If you only wish to receive group invites from friends, check the relevant box on the "Privacy Settings" page of "Account Settings".

Start a group

This is not as hard as you might think. Click "Groups" on the main MySpace navigation bar and then hit the "Create Group" link on the left. Fill in the form, taking care with the various settings that determine how public or private you want the group to be. Lastly, upload an image to represent the group. Job done. You now have your very own group of which you are the almighty moderator – you get to approve any images that are posted by group members and you can also ban any group members who cause trouble or post spam.

To start filling the ranks, click the "Invite Others" link.

MySpace Forums

There is a big overlap between forums (also referred to as bulletin boards or discussion boards) and groups, in that they both feature conversation-like "threads", where an initial topic or question is posted and then anyone can chime in with their own response or idea. But, whereas you might join a group because you have an ongoing interest in a general subject, a forum is somewhere that you might drop by when you need to find the answer to a particular problem. As with groups, the subjects covered are diverse and at times odd, but you will find them particularly useful for the techie stuff – Windows problems, MySpace code issues, etc.

Find a forum

It will take you seconds to grasp the basics – click the "Forum" link on the main MySpace navigation strip and then browse through the various categories for the topic that interests you.

Netiquette

The golden rule of forums and groups, both in MySpace and on the wider Web, is STAY ON SUBJECT. Forums and groups are for discussion, not attention seeking. Nobody wants to find their way to a forum on "comics", "dog food" or whatever, and find it filled with worthless "add me" posts and invitations to "make money quick".

Also, watch your language, be polite and remember that it can often be very easy to misinterpret written sarcasm as aggression. For the full story on so-called "netiquette", check out:
en.wikipedia.org/wiki/Netiquette

11

Events &
calendars

save the date

Joining groups and posting messages in forums
aren't the only ways to communicate with more
than one MySpacer at a time. With the planning and
scheduling options available in MySpace Events, you can
announce all your gigs, parties and happenings to your
friends, or even to the entire MySpace community. Or you
could decide to head out and meet up with some friends
or other like-minded individuals at someone else's event.
And once you've found your share of things to do, you can
use the MySpace calendar functions to help keep all your
dates in order.

MySpace Events

Even if you really enjoy meeting or reconnecting with friends on MySpace, every so often it's nice to get together offline – out in the real world. Whether you're planning a party or just looking to pass some free time, there are options to ease the transition back to reality using MySpace's Events feature.

To begin, click the "Events" link on the main MySpace navigation strip. The "Events Home" will appear and you'll be shown a list of forthcoming events open to the public. From there, use the location search fields to narrow down the list to your local area and the Category dropdown menu to select the sort of event that fits your mood. If a particular outing strikes your fancy, you can RSVP to it and a reminder will automatically be added to your Calendar (see p.110), along with a link to the event.

Create Events

Of course, you're not limited to attending other people's events; you can also plan your own – but you certainly don't have to announce it to everyone on MySpace. Find your way back to the "Events Home" via the navigation strip, and click the "Create Events" link in the top-right corner of the page. Define your event's name, location and category; and, to keep your party off the main Events page, remember to set its type to "private".

Events Links

Event Invites

Events I've Posted

Events I'm Attending

Create New Event

Track your popularity through the Events Links box.

You can then invite specific guests, by selecting them from your Friends list, by typing in their personal email addresses or by searching for them on

My Mail	
🗗 **New Event Invitation!**	
inbox	**friend requests**
sent	**post bulletin**

MySpace. Click "Invite & Update" and a message will be sent out to everyone you've chosen (MySpace members will also receive an "Event Alert" in the "My Mail" box on their Hello page).

Post a bulletin

Another way to reach lots of people at once is by posting a bulletin. Simply click the "Post Bulletin" link in the "My Mail" window of your Hello page, and type your message. After you send the note, an alert will appear in the "My Bulletin Space" on all your friends' Hello pages. Bulletins only last for ten days, so long-term plans are best dealt with in Events.

My Bulletin Space		
From	Date	Bulletin
azul*	Sep 7 2:27 PM	213* September update/ L A to the BAY visitors from the UK!
Sonia	Sep 7 1:07 PM	MK "FALL FLING" KOREAN MATCH-MAKING EVENT @ BLVD...SAT!
azul*	Sep 6 11:14 PM	213* september events-jus for you to enjoy.
Jon Martin	Sep 6 1:56 PM	1, 2, 3, and to tha 4
azul*	Sep 5 1:23 PM	i love me some frohawk
View All Bulletin Entries		

If, after you've posted your bulletin, you realize you've made a mistake – don't fret. It's easy to delete it at any time and write a new one. Simply open the offending post and you're given the option of wiping it away.

Your calendar

You can schedule all manner of events using the MySpace Calendar, which you can then access from any computer connected to the Internet (although, at the time of writing, Safari users were having difficulties seeing their entries). To begin, click either the "Manage Calendar" link in the list next to your photo on your Hello page, or the "My Calendar" link on the MySpace Events page. Then, find the "Options" tab and click through to set your default view and alert options before you start adding appointment entries.

> **Tip:** If you use the calendar for hour-by-hour appointments, the single day view is for you.

Manage your calendar

To add an entry, simply select the date of your event or appointment and click the "add" button. On the next page, you can enter as much or as little information as you want about the appointment – it's a good idea to include at least a title and the time frame. You also have the option to enter repeating appointments, a useful way to set regular weekly meetings, lessons or band rehearsals all at once. Next, decide whether you want a reminder sent to your personal email or MySpace email – if you want one sent at all. And finally, move the privacy bar to your preference. If you choose to share a calendar entry, it will show up in the calendar box on your Hello page, letting your friends and anyone else who views your Profile keep track of your movements.

12
Blogging
welcome to the blogosphere

Even though the success of MySpace is founded upon one-on-one interaction, your opinions need not be limited to posting individual comments on Profile pages. We've already seen how to communicate with lots of people at once using Groups (see p.103), Forums (see p.104) and the MySpace Events feature (see p.107), but if you want your own personal online soapbox, then you need a blog. This chapter explores the basics of blogging on MySpace, and for those of you already familiar with basic blogging tools, it reveals the unique potential of MySpace blogs made possible by the system's "nearly" open source format.

What is blogging?

Blogging is simply the act of posting your thoughts onto a journal-like webpage called a "blog" (short for "weblog"). Those thoughts don't have to be constrained to words – blog posts can include pictures, music and even videos. Like your Profile, every MySpace blog can be viewed by anyone, even non-members, unless you adjust the "Privacy Setting" of each new post. Even then, you should be very careful about what you reveal on your blog, whether it's personal information or a swipe at your employer. You never know who's out there keeping tabs.

Search for blogs

The quickest way to understand what blogs are all about is to uncover a few examples, and MySpace gives you more than one way to dig. The first is by using the search feature available through the "Search" link on the main navigation bar: choose "Blogs" from the dropdown menu and enter your preferred search terms to narrow the results. You can also find top blogs via the "Blog Control Center", which is accessed via either the "Manage Blog" link next to your Hello page picture or the "Blog" link on the MySpace navigation bar. From there, you'll have the option to "View Most Popular Blogs" – these are generally postings by celebrities or those with thousands of people in their Friends list.

In the "Blog Control Center", there's a column of options for writing and managing your favourite reads. For now we'll focus on reading, so note the "My Blog Groups" box at the bottom. You can use the "Browse Blog Groups" option to find other sets of people that share your interests. Just select your preferred subject

Blog Control Center

MySpace Blog
Blog Home
My Subscriptions
My Readers
My Preferred List

sean

	Today	Week	Total
Posts	1	3	45
Comments	5	21	154
Views	14	152	663
Kudos	10	38	280

My Controls
Post New Blog
View Blog
Customize Blog
Blog Safe Mode

My Blog Groups
Browse Blog Groups
Create a Blog Group

and click "Total Members" to find the most populated groups.

Subscribe to a blog

Once you've found a blog you like, you'll probably want to return to it from time to time. There's no need to memorize the address if you choose to subscribe. Just hit the "Subscribe" link at the top right of the blog, and it will be added to your "My Subscriptions" page (which has a link in your "Blog Control Center"). Now, every time that blog is updated, you'll receive a mailbox alert.

 New Blog Subscription Posts!

If you regularly read a list of blogs from a variety of sources outside of MySpace, you probably use an aggregator to manage your subscriptions. If that's the case and you want to keep all your alerts in the same place, you can use the "RSS" link at the top of a MySpace blog to reveal a page of text representing an RSS (really simple syndication) feed. If you enter the address of this page into your aggregator, it will also monitor the MySpace blog for you. If you don't have an aggregator, try:

AmphetaDesk www.disobey.com/amphetadesk
Bloglines www.bloglines.com
Google Reader www.google.com/reader

welcome to MySpace

Blog in MySpace

Though blogs include images, music and video, it's the writing that may seem the most arduous task – but, then again, you probably won't be blogging to pay the bills. Only a handful of bloggers make a living from their pages, and most blogs get started by normal folks just so they can get their opinions out into the ether. So don't beat yourself up over grammar and minor details, but do give it a spell check, please. Additionally, think carefully about what you post and whether it might come back to haunt you.

Change the appearance of your blog

MySpace blogs give you a style sheet with loads of formatting options and colour choices. In your "Blog Control Center", click the "Customize Blog" link in the "My Controls" box. You'll be taken to a page with a long list of tabs and fields, which control different page elements and allow you to customize your blog. For a full description of each of these features, check out the MySpaceBlog'r website (listed below).

You're not limited to the built-in options, either. If you prefer, manipulate your blog's appearance using the same sort of HTML goodies that you use for your Profile page (see p.123).

MySpaceBlog'r www.myspaceblogr.com

> **Tip:** In the colour palettes selection box, don't feel limited to the pre-determined colours. Enter your own values for Red, Green and Blue, and the variations will appear in the swatch to the right.

The Advanced Editor makes it easy to alter the colours, fonts and layout of individual blog posts without the need for manually entering any HTML code.

Post an entry

To get started, log in to MySpace and then hit the "Blog" link on the MySpace navigation bar. Next, click "Post New Blog" within the "My Controls" panel on the left.

Blog posts consist of two parts: the "subject" and the "body". The subject is like a newspaper headline. Use it to grab attention and draw readers in. The body is the meat of your post, and it can be composed of text, images or music (to find out how to embed music into your MySpace pages, see p.128). If you don't have a PC running Internet Explorer, you won't be able to use the Advanced Editor (above), but the basic editor provides some help with inserting images and Web links. And you can always change your font style and format using common HTML tags (see p.125).

> **Tip:** Whenever you write a new blog post, be sure to set your desired privacy setting for that specific entry using the radio buttons at the bottom of the "Post A New Blog Entry" page.

> **Tip:** If you use Firefox (see p.33), you might consider downloading "Performancing" for Firefox – a MySpace blog editor that sits in your browser. For the download, head to: addons.mozilla.org/firefox/3229

Podcasts and vodcasts

Blogging purists will tell you that posting some downloadable music or video on your blog doesn't mean you're podcasting, though you're certainly able to post these sorts of files in your blog (see Chapters 16 & 17 for more on this). To truly podcast or video-cast (vodcast), you'll need to attach an RSS feed to your media file, and then use some code to make the feed appear in your blog. Ideally, the "Podcast Enclosure" field at the bottom of the MySpace blog editor would do this for you – unfortunately it is very buggy, and users almost unanimously report that it refuses to work.

Still, you have options. While a full description of creating podcasts or vodcasts is outside the scope of this book, if you already have some self-created audio or video files saved on a server somewhere, you can create an RSS feed for them manually (see www.audiofeeds.org/tutorial.php). Alternatively, you might try one of these automatic RSS feed generators:

FeedBurner www.feedburner.com
Liberated Syndication www.libsyn.com
Podomatic www.podomatic.com

You can also embed an audio podcast player using:

Odeo www.odeo.com/channel/6641/embedded_player
PicklePlayer www.podcastpickle.com/app/player/free.php

13

More MySpace

last but not least...

As has been said again and again in this book, MySpace can be almost anything to anyone, if they are willing to define their own little bit of the landscape – perhaps by setting up a blog (see p.111) or group (see p.103), or by sharing their thoughts in forums (see p.103) or by posting bulletins (p.109). However, there are also some very broad communities within MySpace. Beyond their massive memberships, the feature that sets these wider communities apart is the fact that MySpace gives each of them specific features and a special place along the ever-present MySpace main navigation bar.

MySpace Music

MySpace and music have always gone hand-in-hand. If you want to take a look at the seemingly limitless arena of acts and artists from every genre, click the "Music" link on the MySpace navigation bar and then start burrowing. For the full story on MySpace Music, turn to p.167.

> **Tip:** While browsing MySpace Music pages, if you come across a track you like so much you want to add it to your own Profile page, simply click the "Add" button.

MySpace Film

Though by no means as established as the Music community, MySpace's Film community is ever-expanding. As well as providing Profile pages for both aspiring independent filmmakers and established names (much like MySpace Music), this community boasts a plethora of extras: film forums, local listings for screenings and even classified ads for jobs in the movie industry.

The "Advanced Search" function in this part of the site is also a little different; it helps you track down filmmakers not only by name, but also by country, location, role (director, editor, animator, etc), keyword and several other search fields from filmmak-

> **Tip:** If it's videos you're after, try typing vids.myspace.com into your Web browser. A little like YouTube.com, here you'll find everything from pop promos and interviews to *Jackass*-style shockers. For more on MySpace Video, see p.157.

Use the drop-down menu under "Advanced Search" to narrow your film-maker searches.

ers' Profile pages. The film community is worth a visit if only for the sheer volume of otherwise-impossible-to-find film trailers that have been made available as streaming video.

MySpace Books

At the time of writing, the "Books" community link appears in a box just below the main navigation strip on the MySpace homepage. From there, you can click through to numerous book groups and read entries from featured blogs. There is also a chart of so-called "top books" with links to where to buy them online.

MySpace Games

The link to "Games" can also be found in the box below the navigation strip on the MySpace homepage. It includes loads of games you can play online, from classic arcade laser-fests to quizzes and puzzles, and also games you can download – some for free and some for a fee. The most interesting feature is that you can challenge other MySpacers to battle you at your chosen game.

MySpace Schools

The "Schools" link in the same box on the MySpace homepage offers a quick way through to the charts listing the most popular school community groups on MySpace, and also allows you to search for your own school (covered in detail on p.81).

MySpace Comedy

Also recently added to the circus is MySpace Comedy. You can watch sketches, click through to joke forums and sign yourself up as a comedian. There is also a great "Advanced Search" feature to help you track down the laughs.

Part 3

Make it your own

14

Pimp your Profile

it's all in the code

Many readers may well have jumped straight to this section of the book before looking at anything else. And why not – this is where the fun starts and those creative juices start flowing. Whether you have been using MySpace for a while, or are a newbie reading this book from cover to cover, you will by now have realised that the secret ingredient in any unique MySpace profile is the HTML code behind the page. You may also have gleaned from your time online that many MySpacers have little idea how to use HTML well. This chapter offers the basics of "hacking" your MySpace code alongside a few golden rules of webpage design.

make it your own

What is HTML code?

HTML is an acronym for HyperText Markup Language, which, despite its intimidating name, is actually not too hard to get on with. In short, HTML is the code used to style and position the text, images and other components within a webpage. And your MySpace Profile page is basically a webpage just like any other. When anyone views your Profile, their Web browser reads the code and works out how to display the contents of the page. Equally, whenever you add any information to your Profile page via the various online forms (see p.68) you are in fact editing and adding to the HTML backbone of the page.

A quick CSS primer

Equally as important as HTML code these days is CSS code, where "CSS" stands for "Cascading Style Sheet". These style sheets are normally separate files that contain all sorts of page-styling information, from font size and colour to text alignment. Subsequently, any HTML code you write can draw upon the styles you've defined, saving you loads of tedious page formatting work. Building your own style sheets is very easy as, like HTML files, they can be created in a basic text editor and then saved with a ".css" file extension.

Each style sheet is made up of "rules", that look something like this:

h2 { color: #FFFFFF }

This rule states that text in our HTML code that is tagged as "h2" will be white, the hex colour code (see p.126) for white being "FFFFFF". Simple. The style sheet can either be referenced in your HTML as a seperate CSS file or embedded within the page itself.

As with HTML, you don't have to do any of the work yourself if you don't want to, as "code generators" can do everything for you. If you do fancy having a crack at it, try one of the many tutorials to be found online. Here's a good place to start: www.w3.org/Style/CSS/

Yet, you don't have to learn HTML to build a MySpace Profile page, because there are many online resources – so called "code generators" – that will do the techie bit for you (more on these later). However, at some point you'll probably need to go in and tweak the raw code, so it is worth knowing the basics.

What's more, the webpages of many other online communities, such as Bebo and Friendster, employ customizable HTML code in their pages, so much of what is said here is also applicable to them.

Get to grips with code

HTML code (often simple refered to as "code" in MySpace circles) is much simpler than computer programming in general, and it only takes a few hours to learn the basics. The next time you're on MySpace, examine the raw code that makes up any

Colour codes

Once you start using code on your MySpace Profile, you'll soon notice that colours are represented by a six-figure string, known as the "hexadecimal colour code". They tend to comprise numbers, though certain letters do also crop up; white, for example, has the code #FFFFFF (note that these hexadecimal colour codes always appear in lines of code with a hash (#) in front of them.

For many years it was understood that there were only 216 so called "safe" hexadecimal colours that could be used online – colours that would look smooth (were non-"dithering") and would display identically across all platforms and on all monitors. Today, computer screens do a better job of displaying many more colours, so we have a much wider choice as page designers. That said, there will still be people out there viewing your Profile page on older machines. For a quick reference of the various safe colour codes, check out: html-color-codes.com

Arguably the most important rule of webpage design is make sure the colours work. There are few things more annoying than coming to a MySpace profile page which features very dark grey text on a black background (apologies to all goths and death metal bands out there, but it can't be read!). Equally, combining dayglo text and a multicoloured background pattern is not going to increase the size of your Friends list. Especially when nobody can even find the "Add to Friends" link.

Even if you're certain you have an especially keen eye for design, try different combinations of colours before you make a final decision. AND BE SURE IT'S READABLE. There are tons of colour resources online that'll help you make better choices and show you which combinations of colours work best. There are several suggested 4-colour schemes in the inside-front-cover of this book, and a great complementary colour selection tool to be found online at: www.siteprocentral.com/html_color_code.html

To find out the "hex" code for colours you want to use, say from a picture on your computer screen, get your hands on a colour-picking application. In OS X use the built-in DigitalColor Meter, which can be found in the Applications/ Utilities folder (select "RGB As Hex Value, 8-bit" setting from the dropdown menu). Windows users download the free Color Detector utility from: www.cosmin.com/colordetector

Profile page – choose to view the "Source" from your browser's View menu. The first thing you'll notice is that the text is surrounded with comments enclosed between less-than and greater-than symbols, like this:

<b>Welcome to my Profile page</b>

These comments are known as tags. In the example above, the tags would make the text "Welcome to my Profile page" appear bold. Most tags come in pairs and apply to the text they enclose. A tag featuring a forward slash signals the end of a pair of tags' relevance, as in: </b>

Here are some common code tags that you may want to use:

Italics <i>your text</i>
Underline <u>your text</u>
Text size <font size=4>your text</font>
Text color <font color=#FFFFFF>your text</font>
Align Left <div align="left">your text</div>
Align Right <div align="right">your text</div>
Centered <center>your text</center>
Web link <a href="www.yourlink.com">your text</a>

And some more that work singularly; ie, they don't require a pairing tag:

Line break
New paragraph <p>
Horizontal rule <hr>

At its most simple, therefore, creating code for a MySpace page is just a matter of sandwiching text between the necessary tags and placing it in a profile field.

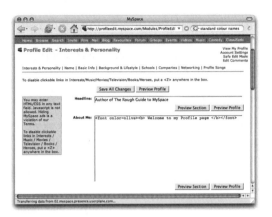

And what's more, you can rack up the tags on either side of your text to add as many attributes as you want. In the example pictured above, the text "Welcome to my Profile page" is enclosed between a pair of bolding tags and a pair of font colour tags that force the text to be displayed in the colour "olive" (see Tip box opposite).

Creating links

If you want to include links to pictures, video, MP3 files, or other websites for that matter, you need to have the relevant file hosted (which means stored online, see p.154) somewhere and then "point to it" using special pairs of tags in the code. Many hosting sites will generate this code for you when files are deposited on their servers, but it's still worth knowing the basics.

> **Tip:** For more help with HTML code and some fine tutorials, visit: www.myspace.com/profilesupport

> **Tip:** As well as the hexadecimal colour codes there are sixteen standard colour names that can be used in your code: "aqua", "black", "blue", "fuchsia", "gray", "green", "lime", "maroon", "navy", "olive", "purple", "red", "silver", "white", "yellow" and "teal" (which I am sure you will be delighted to learn is a rather pleasant greeny/blue colour that takes its name from a small duck).

Example #1

To link the word "badger" to the Rough Guides homepage and have it open in the same browser window:

```
<a href=http://www.roughguides.com>badger</a>
```

To create the same link but have it open in a new browser window, change the opening tag to:

```
<a href=http://www.roughguides.com target="_blank">
```

Example #2

And don't feel limited to just using text on your Profile page. Any field that you can paste a link into can be used to display an image. In this example, the image "dog.jpg" is stored on "www.myserver.com". Note the inclusion of a "border" code, which determines whether the image will appear with or without a frame.

```
<img src=http://www.myserver.com/dog.jpg border="0">
```

Taking this example a step further, the code can be expanded so that the image itself becomes a link to the Rough Guides homepage, and by pasting the code into the appropriate field of the MySpace "Edit Profile" form, the image can be made to

make it your own

appear in a specific place on the page ... under the "About Me" heading for example:

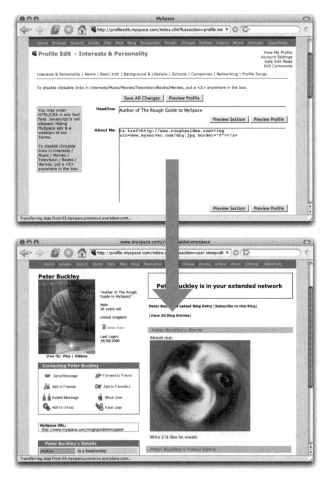

So, that's the very least you need to know to get started with MySpace code. There are literally millions of things that you can do with code, so if you have an idea in your head, search online for either a tutorial to show you how to achieve it, or some ready-made code that's just waiting to be used. For information about the best places to look, turn to p.216.

Layout generators

So far, this chapter has only examined a few scraps of HTML code, but what many users want is a one-stop-shop that'll do all the hard work and spit out the code for an entire Profile page – enter, "the layout generator". There are loads of generators to be found online and most work in the same way. You click through a bunch of options regarding text colours, link colours, background colours, table colours, etc. At the end of the process, the generator offers a large wad of code that you copy (Ctrl+C or Apple+C) and paste (Ctrl+V or Apple+V) into the "About Me" field of your MySpace "Edit Profile" page.

This code embeds a CSS (Cascading Style Sheet, see p.124) into your Profile page; the style sheet defines the attributes for all the elements of your page. And you can still add any text you want to your "About Me" field after the code.

Some generators are easier to use than others (there are links

Tip: The code from many layout generators will include a link to the generator's website; this link will more than likely appear somewhere on your Profile page. If you don't want it there, feel free to edit the link out of the code after you've pasted it into the "Edit Profile" form.

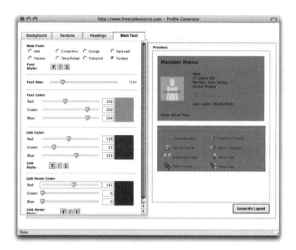

to a few of the best below; also see p.216) and some offer more features than others. Even with a generator it can be a bit of a hit and miss exercise, so don't lose heart if it takes a bit of toing and froing before you get the exact look that you want.

FreeCodeSource.com www.freecodesource.com
GameSpot www.gamedspot.com
Pimp-My-Profile.com www.pimp-my-profile.com
YourCoolProfile.com www.yourcoolprofile.com

A word of warning about many online code sites. Though they'll help you get the job done, these kind of sites have a nasty habit of throwing pop-up ads at you every time you move between pages. If you can see a "Skip" button, hit it whenever possible, and never agree to download any software or plug-ins. To be extra safe while cruising these sites, read the advice on p.32.

If you find it all a little too "in ya face", your best port of call

Good design, bad design

Because there's more than enough room in online communities for everyone who wants to publish a homepage or Profile page, and absolutely no means of enforcing any kind of quality control, sites like MySpace have become a haven for design and content that's impossible to digest – dayglo pink text against a bright green background, for example, complete with distracting flashing images and fancy mouse cursors. So, before you even get near any layout generator tools, think about how you want your page to look and who your audience is, and try not to make the same mistakes that others have made on the World Wide Web:

Bad Design Features www.ratz.com/featuresbad.html
Web Pages That Suck www.webpagesthatsuck.com
Worst Of The Web www.worstoftheweb.com

The point of your page is to convey some message about yourself, and you surely don't want to come off as completely tasteless, so at the very least be certain your pages are easy to read. Almost all the most successful Profile pages stick to a similar minimal structure. The buzzword for this is "usability". You can read all about it here:

SpiderPro StyleGuide www.spiderpro.com/pr/pri.html
Usable Web www.usableweb.com
WebWord Usability Weblog www.webword.com

Try Vischeck on Your Image Files

Select the type of color vision to simulate:

- Deuteranope (a form of red/green color deficit)
- Protanope (another form of red/green color deficit)
- Tritanope (a blue/yellow deficit- very rare)

Image file: [   ] Browse...
Run Vischeck!

If, after all that, you're still considering a patterned background image (see p.136), at least spare a thought for the colour-blind:

Vischeck www.vischeck.com

make it your own

Tip: Never be talked into exchanging cash for MySpace codes – there's more than enough free stuff out there to go around.

could be the basic-looking, but effective StrikeFile layout code generator:

Strikefile www.strikefile.com/myspace

Off-the-peg layouts

Most of the sites already listed offer a plethora of weird, wild and crazy additions to your MySpace Profile (some of which are covered in the following chapter). Many also offer ready-to-roll Profile page layout codes. You simply browse a catalogue of layout thumbnails – often arranged by colour or category – choose the one you like, grab the code and paste it into your "Edit Profile" form.

Customizing other networks

Bebo Skins beboskins.net
FreeFever.com www.freefever.com/hi5
Friendster Layouts friendster-layouts.com
Friendster Tweaker friendster-tweakers.com
Hi5Love.com www.hi5love.com

15 top
hacks

make your MySpace stand out

So, now you know the basics … it's all in the code. Over the next few pages this chapter will make suggestions for changes and additions you might want to make to your MySpace Profile, from placing a background image and loading a music player on your page, to creating spangling glitter text and creating your own personalized "Zwinky". Now, before you get carried away, let me point out that if you made every modification to your Profile that this chapter suggests, you would be left with a outlandish and unreadable creation that wouldn't do your Friends List any favours at all. So go easy.

#1 Change your MySpace background

All MySpace Profile pages comprise the same basic structure – a table of boxes that sits atop a background. Most MySpace layout generators (see p.131) offer the option to set either a colour for this background or to use an image in the background. This background image can either be used just once (in which case it needs to be big enough to span the full width and height of your page, see p.150), or tiled to create a patterned effect. For hundreds of examples and the code to make it happen, visit:

Backgrounds Archive backgroundsarchive.com

If you want to use your own image, then you'll have to get it hosted (see p.154) and either build the code using a layout generator (see p.131), find a host that offers specific code for placing background images, or write your own. This online tutorial will show you how: www.simpletidbits.com/blog/category/internet/myspace/adding-a-background

#2 Flip it

Be the envy of your friends by flipping your Profile page – you'll end up with your personal information on the right and all your comments, friends list, etc, on the left. Stick this CSS code into your "About Me" field and the job's done:

```
<style type="text/css">table {direction:rtl;}
table table table {direction:ltr;}</style>
```

If you already have a style sheet in your "About Me" field, simply edit the "direction:rtl;" and "direction:ltr;" attributes into the "table" and "table table table" lines of the code respectively.

#3 Add background music

These days anyone can have music playing on their Profile page, not just people with MySpace Music accounts. Log yourself in and then click the "Music" link in the main MySpace navigation strip. From here, find the Profile page of a band whose music you want to add to your Profile page and click the "Add" button next to the favoured song on their MP3 music player – it'll be added to your Profile in a strip just below the "Contacting…" and "MySpace URL" boxes.

Then, from your "Account Settings" page, click the "Music Settings" link to edit the way the music behaves when your Profile page is viewed.

You only get one song at a time on your Profile page, so if you hit an "add" button on a different MySpace Music Profile page, the new song will replace any previous selection. If a song you like features an un-clickable "add" button, it means that the artist has not enabled that feature on their Profile (see tip below).

> **Tip:** Musicians. To allow people to add your music to their page on MySpace, click "Edit Profile" on your Hello page and then go to the "Manage Songs" tab. Check the "Allow users to add songs to their profile" option and then click the "Update Settings" button.

#4 Add a profile counter

MySpace does provide you with information about the volume of hits that your Profile page receives, but it is for your eyes only – to be found in the right-hand panel on your Hello page. If you want to add a counter to your public Profile, so that everyone else can see how busy your page is, get your hands on the codes to be found at: www.killerkiwi.net/myspace/counter

31 Aug 2006
Your Network: 105,978,073
Profile Views: 6
Last Login: 31/08/2006
Show My: **Ranking Score** **Favourites** **Invite History** **Classified Posts** **Bulletin Posts** **My Groups**

#5 Create a MySpace scroller

Using the idiot-proof online code-generating utility found at www.freezark.com/scroller/index.php, you can create a very nice looking, retro, LED-style scrolling message to plaster across your Profile page.

#6 Create a slideshow

Slideshows are a great way to post loads of images on your Profile page in one fell swoop. They can do a range of things, from creating banners of images that scroll from left to right, to making fully integrated and captioned little movies that look a little like PowerPoint presentations. The easiest way to get the job done is with a specialized image host service that helps you build a slideshow and then provides you with the necessary code.

MySpaceSlideshow www.myspaceslideshow.net/create.php
Slide www.slide.com/arrange
Sliderole www.slideroll.com/slideshows/myspace

make it your own

#7 Customize your "Contact..." box

The "Contact..." box in your Profile is probably the most frequently used section of your page, and yet it's the blandest in appearance. Luckily, there are code sites that can help you replace the default design with a sparky little box built from any number of patterns and styles.

Just make sure that the design you choose complements the rest of your Profile's content, otherwise it'll stick out like a sore thumb. You could even take the track of choosing your "Contact..." box first, and basing the rest of your colour scheme on it.

Tabwin www.tabwin.com

Alternatively, you can generate a design using your own background image with the generator found at:

Muttie.com www.muttie.com/generators/contact-box-code.php

Bad karma

Just so you know, here are a couple of things that you can't do with your Profile page. MySpace does not allow any MySpace trackers (programs that monitor where people are coming from when they visit your Profile, and going to when they leave). If you are caught using one, your account will be deleted. Equally, hacks for removing the banner ads at the top of your MySpace Profile page, though easy to deploy, are a no-no.

#8 Create a Zwinky

Zwinkies are kookie little cartoon representations of yourself that'll sit on your MySpace Profile page and generally look cute. SmileCentral offers a very slick tool for their production:

SmileCentral zwinky.smileycentral.com

#9 Create an MP3 player

MySpace allows you to add one song by a MySpace artist to your Profile page, but without too much trouble you can create a fully functioning MP3 player that will let people listen to a selection of songs on your page. Music can be a great way to show people what you are about, and these types of player can reveal a large slice of your taste. The code is a little more involved, and you will have to find somwehere online to host the song files that you want to stream through the player, but there are loads of tutorials online and even a few MySpace Groups dedicated to the subject. One of the best players up for grabs can be found here:

Jeroen's Player
www.jeroenwijering.com/?item=Flash_MP3_Player

The best thing about these kind of Flash Players is that you get to choose the exact "skin", or appearance, of the device when you create the code.

#10 Tweak your Profile's layout

By default, the MySpace Profile page is a cluttered creature, and many of the items you see spread out before you might either be surplus to requirement or, in your opinion, would look much better in some other position on the page.

Because every item's position is determined by the code behind the page, it's all relatively easy to rearrange. If you already know your HTML inside out, dive straight in and reposition the boxes and lists

at will. If you are not so confident, then look online for the individual pieces of code dealing with each page element. The TweakingMySpace website is a good place to start; there you can pick up code for everything from centring all the elements on your page to creating scrollable friends and comment lists.

TweakingMySpace tweakingmyspace.rockmyprofile.com/Tweaks

As a quick example, try pasting the simple piece of code below to the end of the "I'd Like to Meet" field, under "Interests & Personality" on your "Edit Profile" page. It will centre your friends and comments lists at the bottom of your Profile page ... easy.

```
</table></tr></td>
```

#11 Add a custom cursor

If you think your viewers might appreciate a change from having their mouse pointer hovering over your page as a humble little arrow, add some code to customize the "cursor" so it will appear in a fanciful fash-ion when anyone visits your page. A quick Google search will reveal thousands of available graphics, ranging from the sleek to the down right daft.

#12 Add Flash Games

There's more fun to be had with this little hack than you can shake a stick at. Visit one of the sites listed below, copy some code, paste it into your "Edit Profile" page, and before you know it you have an intergalactic shoot-'em-up installed on your Profile.

BunchBall www.bunchball.com
FreeBlogGames www.freebloggames.com
MySpaceArcade www.myspacearcade.com

#13 Add an audio comments system

This genius idea comes in the form of MyChingo. It's basically a voicemail system for your MySpace Profile, blog, or any other website you might have. Assuming your visitors have a microphone connected to their computer they can leave you messages and comments in the form of MP3s. You can then choose whether you want these messages to be public or private.

If you sign up for the free version of the service, the messages you receive can be anything up to two minutes long, but if you are willing to part with a little cash, both the monthly ($3.95) and annual ($45) subscriptions allow you to collect messages of up to half an hour in length. If you want to avoid accruing hours and hours of mindless drivel, it's probably best just to stick with the free version.

MyChingo www.mychingo.com

make it your own

#14 Add some SubTags

SubTags (or Subject Tags) are great fun and add a little extra interaction to your MySpace Profile page. It's a good way to garner public opinion on an issue, or get feedback from an image or video clip. To get started, drop by the SubTags website, sign up (it's free) and choose a "subject" to post to your Profile, this allows people viewing your page to add "tags" to your "subject".

SubTags.com www.subtags.com

#15 Pinch someone else's

Finally, the best way to achieve exactly what you want on your Profile page, whilst simultaneously getting to grips with HTML code, is to pinch another user's code (see p.125).

If you fancy completely duplicating the appearance of another MySpace Profile, then check out the Layout Snatcher listed below. All you need in order to generate the code for the page you have your eye on is the "Friend ID" code – a string of numbers found in the address when you click through to their Profile page from any friends list (if you get to the page by typing the user's URL, the ID will not appear).

Layout Snatcher www.killerkiwi.net/myspace/layout-snatcher

16
Images & photos

getting images online

Whichever community you are aligned with – whether it be MySpace, Bebo, Friendster, or whatever – pictures play an important part of your online day-to-day. They're used as a means of expression, to illustrate blogs and comments, as bulletins, and so much more. With regard to MySpace you already know how to upload images to the "My Pictures" section of your Profile (see p.64), but do you know how to prepare an image for the Web in the first place? Or host images elsewhere on line? And haven't you always wanted to know how to make animated images? This chapter reveals all.

make it your own

Picture sources

If you really don't have the time to mess around with home-spun images (see below), there are plenty of other sources of images to be found online.

The key is copyright – you shouldn't post images that you do not own the copyright to or do not have permission to use. In short, you can't just skip around the Web pinching any old photo or graphic that you fancy using. The alternative is to search one of the many online public-domain image libraries. But check for any small print before you grab the files you fancy:

Pixel Perfect Digital www.pixelperfectdigital.com
Morgue File www.morguefile.com

There are also numerous sites tailored for the MySpace market that offer free graphics, banners, "funny" images and the like. As you might expect, you'll often have to battle with pop-ups and ads

Creating images from scratch

There are three ways to produce a digital image. First, by taking a photo with a digital camera (or a still from a digital video camera) and importing it into your computer. Second, by using a scanner to import a virtual copy of an existing photograph, drawing or just about anything else two-dimensional. These days, decent-enough digital cameras and scanners can be picked up inexpensively. The third technique is to create images from scratch on your computer using a drawing program. You'll find many such tools for free online, and Windows features its own, very simple tool, called Paint. All of them, however, pale in comparison with professional-level products such as:

Illustrator www.adobe.com/illustrator
CorelDraw www.corel.com

> **Tip:** To copy an image from a webpage (using either a Mac or Windows PC) simply drag it from the browser into an open folder window.

to get at the content, but you may well find something you like, and many such sites will provide you with the necessary code for a specific image, so you don't have to

worry about hosting (see p.154). Try this address for starters:

MyGraphicSpace www.mygraphicspace.com

Image file formats

There are various different file formats that work well online, all of which are basically trying to do the same thing – maximize the image quality while minimizing the file size. Obviously you want your images to look good, but they also need to be small enough

> **Tip:** If you want to change the file format of an image file, or in any way manipulate its appearance, you are going to need some photo editing software (see p.34).

make it your own

Tip: If you are creating or resizing an image for your MySpace background, and you don't want it to "tile", make sure it's wide enough to span most user's browser windows. About 900 pixels should do the trick.

to download quickly and efficiently. That's why you need to know about file formats, because different formats use different types of "compression" to achieve the best quality with the least bytes. And certain formats work better with certain kinds of images.

GIF or JPEG?

The two most popular image formats on the Web are JPEG (.jpg) and GIF (.gif), and these are the only two formats you can use when uploading images to your MySpace "My Pictures" page. GIFs can only display 256 colours, while JPEGs can display millions. JPEGs also permit a greater degree of compression for detailed images. For these two reasons, most photographs are best saved as JPEGs.

GIFs have their uses, though. If an image contains a relatively small number of colours or has large expanses of the same colour, a GIF allows a much smaller file size with little loss of quality. GIFs can also be animated like a slideshow (see below), and can have transparent backgrounds. Consequently, they're often used for bars, icons, banners and backgrounds.

PNG files

PNG is the new kid on the Web images block. This file type is similar to a GIF, but can't be used for animation. It does, however, feature very sophisticated transparency support.

Animated GIFs

Ever seen those thumbnail images in your friends list that flash repeatedly or show a simple, flip book-ish sequence? Well they are animated GIFs. To many they are the scourge of the Internet – both irritating and pointless. But they can also be fun and, if used subtlety, can make your Profile page look very cool. Again, there are tons of ready-made files to be found online from sites ready to exchange a GIF for a link back to their homepage. Gifs. net is as good a resource as any:

Gifs.net www.gifs.net

If you want to make your own animated GIFs, try the fully-featured GIFmation (for both Mac and PC). Download the free demo from: www.boxtopsoft.com/gifmation.html. Animated GIFs can also be created using the wonderful, and free, GIMP.

GIMP www.gimp.org

Prepare your images

Preparing graphics can turn out to be half the fun of making your home within an online community. First, there's the issue of getting photos and other "artwork" to look right. Second, there's the skill of creating images that are integral to the design of the

Tip: Not sure what dimensions you need your image to be? Why not look for an image on MySpace that displays at roughly the size you want, copy it to your computer and open it in your image editor to find out its dimensions.

A Web search for "MySpace thank you" reveals a wealth of animated graphics to use in response to positive comments.

make it your own

page. It's worth noting that you can use images to do some pretty creative things with words too. Look online and you'll find that lots of "text" actually consists of images – as this allows people to use any font and special effect they want.

Reducing an image's file size

Before you post a digital image on the Web, you'll probably need to reduce its size in bytes, otherwise it will take an age to download. You can do this in two ways – both of which will need some kind of image-editing software (see p. 34).

▶ **Reduce the dimensions** of the image in pixels, making the picture itself smaller. For example, if it measures 1024x768 pixels, you could reduce it to, say, 800x600. You could also crop the image, chopping off excess from the edges. These techniques will change the size and shape of the image, but not otherwise affect the quality.

> **Tip:** Whenever you compress a file, you run the risk of losing quality. So, rather than make incremental changes to the compressed image, complete any touch-ups and cropping in the original format, and then export images with different levels of compression from that master version. But be sure to keep a copy of your original image.

▶ **Compress the image** Compressed image formats such as JPEG and GIF allow an image to be made much smaller in terms of file size. If you compress too much, however, the reduced file size will come at the cost of image quality – things might start to look blocky or blurred. Done right, however, the compressed version will look identical to the naked eye but will be much smaller in terms of file size. When you save or resave a compressed image in an image editing program (see p.34), you can select from various different compression levels, allowing you to try various options and strike a good balance between image quality and file size.

> **Tip:** When naming images for use online, keep the file names short and without any special characters or spaces.

> **Tip:** Also worth checking out is a free PC application called IrfanView. It can be used to quickly resave images so they are less than 600k – the maximum file size that you are allowed to upload to the "My Pictures" area of your Profile.

Posting and hosting

As has been said, the "My Pictures" (see p.64) section of your Profile is not the only place you can dump images on MySpace. Anywhere that code can be added, you can type or paste a link to an image stored (or "hosted") somewhere online. That allows you the option of placing images pretty much anywhere on your Profile page, and also within your blog entries, in bulletins, and within the comment fields on other people's pages. It also means

> **Tip:** Image host code generators often include a link back to their site in the code they provide; feel free to remove it from the code before you paste it into your Profile page.

you can push the boat out and post images larger than 600k – the maximum size that MySpace allows – assuming you can find a host site willing to harbour your larger files.

Image hosts

This process is made all the more easy by the plethora of image hosting services that have sprung up in recent years as a result of the explosion in popularity of online communities. You simply choose your host site, upload your image, and paste the provided image code into your Profile page. There's no such thing as a free lunch however, and most services include a link to their page within the provided code, thus increasing their own traffic with click-throughs from your page. If you do use any of these services, check the user agreements, as some may only host your

> **Tip:** Always keep a back-up copy of any images that you've left with a host; then, if there are problems with the host site, you can simply stick the images somewhere else and replace the code on your Profile page.

> **Tip:** If you host your own images, you are going to have to generate your own codes. To see how it's done, turn to "Example #2" on p.129.

images for a set period and, obviously, when your time is up, the code on your page will stop working. Here are a few hosts worth checking out:

FotoDunk www.fotodunk.com
Image Dump www.imgdump.net
ImageShack imageshack.us
MySpace Support www.myspacesupport.com/image-host

Flickr

Loads of people ask about displaying images on their MySpace pages that they have posted with Flickr (www.flickr.com), the largest online photo storage community. At the time of writing, the two communities are pretty incompatible; and given that Flickr is now owned by Yahoo! (who have their own Yahoo! 360° community, which already integrates the service, see p.20), the situation seems unlikely to change very soon. That said, it is possible to create a slideshow of Flickr images by using the service provided at www.slide.com (see p.139).

make it your own

Photo Ranking

And finally, a brief word on a popular MySpace feature called "Photo Ranking", where by you make one or more of your images available for anyone looking at your Profile page to mark out of ten. It's not a new idea on the Internet, and can be traced back to the now infamous www.hotornot.com website. Be warned though, a person does NOT have to be your friend to comment, so you are opening yourself up to attack. Here's what you can do:

▶ **To submit your image** to the Ranking system, click "Upload / Change photos" on your Hello page and then click the "Add My Picture" button below the picture you want added.

▶ **To view your ranking** click the "Ranking Score" link in the right-hand panel of your Hello page. You can remove your images from the rating system at any time.

▶ **To rank someone else** click the "Rank User" link in the "Contacting..." box of their Profile page. From here you can also view the "Top Ranked" people on MySpace and even home in on a particular geographical area.

▶ **To rank at random** click the "Skip" button on the rankings page to be taken to image after image of random victims.

Before submitting your images for ranking it's worth taking a look at some of the comments on the images of "Top Ranked" MySpacers ... it'll probably put you off pretty quickly. You can also protect yourself to a degree by returning to your Hello page, clicking "Account Settings", and then enabling the "Privacy Settings" option that reads "Approve Comments before Posting" (see p.97).

17
Video clips
movies and MySpace

These days pretty much anyone can make a video and post it on the Web for the world to see – you don't need anything more complicated than a mobile phone with video-capability and access to a computer. And you most certainly don't need any talent ... far more useful might be ownership of a singing rabbit or the ability to fall over a bush while juggling. Of course, video clips also have serious uses, most notably video blogging, which can also be done through MySpace. That said, the idea of an online community where you can post "streaming" video clips (clips that you play, or stream, from the webpage via a video player embedded on the page) is not new and MySpace is going to have to run very fast to catch up with YouTube.com – without a doubt the largest video-posting community out there. This chapter will help you get started with video, whichever community you are a part of.

How to make a video

The hardest part of the whole video production process is trying to find something that is actually worth posting online. Browse the various categories lurking behind the "Videos" link on the main MySpace navigation bar to get a feel for what's already there. You'll find everything from pop promos

from established stars that have been posted by fans, to footage of toddlers taking their first steps and cats being sickeningly cute.

There are also plenty of MySpacers who spend their free time re-enacting their favourite scenes from the movies, complete with special effects, monsters, light sabres … the works.

Video hardware

To get started you need a device such as a DV camcorder, digital camera, webcam or mobile phone – anything that can shoot digital movies and offers a means of transferring the footage onto

> **Tip:** Though you can find tons of live music video footage in MySpace Videos that you may not get a chance to see elsewhere, for official pop promos go to the dedicated video section of MySpace Music (see p.185).

More video sources

There are other ways to source video footage for your creations other than filming it yourself. In brief, you can also:

▶ **Import footage from a file** This option is generally found in the "File" menu of video editing packages and lets you browse for existing files on either your computer, a connected drive, or a data CD or DVD.

▶ **Ripped DVDs** Though there are obvious legal issues regarding the ripping of commercial DVDs, you may well have your own holiday footage, or the like, on a DVD that you want to re-edit and post online. Windows users can do the job with Flash DVD Ripper ($35 from www.dvd-ripper.com), while Apple owners are best served by HandBrake (download it for free from hand-brake.m0k.org) which rips the footage into a format such as MPEG-4 that can then be imported straight into iMovie (see overleaf).

▶ **Video grabs** This is a moving-image verison of a regular screenshot, recording whatever is happening on your screen to a video file – even if it's streaming from the Web. Try Display Eater on a Mac (www.reversecode.com) or Replay Screencast on a PC (www.applian.com/replay-screencast).

▶ **Photographs** iMovie (see overleaf) lets you transform still images into video clips, but it can also be done using CameraMover (www.info-services.net/cameramover) on a Mac and Image Video Machine (www.dandans.com/ImageVideoMachine.htm) on a PC.

your computer. Most devices will more than likely come bundled with all the software you need to transfer, or "capture", your raw footage, though you may also be able to manage the capture process using either of the editing applications described overleaf.

Tip: If you are a Mac user and don't get along with the video capture software built into iMovie, you might consider using the Pro version of Apple's QuickTime player as a video capture tool: www.quicktime.com

Video editing software

Of course, you could simply upload your video clips as they are, but it's far more fun and satisfying to edit them first, with software such as iMovie HD (shipped with all Macs sold in the last few years) or Windows Movie Maker (if your Version of Windows XP doesn't have it, download Service Pack 2 from Microsoft). As well as chopping the actual footage, these applications will help you add titles and special effects. For more information and resources, visit:

iMovie HD www.apple.com/ilife
Windows Movie Maker www.microsoft.com/moviemaker

> **Tip:** Most video clips posted on MySpace have a resolution (in pixels) of 320x240. This is the same size as a Video iPod screen. As such, you can also use iTunes to convert existing movie files to a format (.m4v) that'll work online (though the file size will be weightier). Drag the file into iTunes, highlight it, and choose "Convert Selection for iPod" from the "Advanced" menu.

Video formats

MySpace accepts a bewildering selection of file formats (anything with one of the following file extensions is acceptable: .asf, .wmv, .mov, .qt, .3g2, .3gp, .3gp2, .3gpp, .gsm, .mpg, .mpeg, .mp4, .m4v, .mp4v, .cmp, .divx, .xvid, .264, .rm, .rmvb, .flv). However, if you are working with the video editing software mentioned above, you should end up outputting either Windows Media Video files (.WMV) from Movie Maker or A QuickTime movie file (.mov) from iMovie HD (see box).

You will soon discover when looking at the output options available, that video formating can be a complicated business, and as well as the actual file format, you can set parameters for numerous things, including frame-rate (per second), the audio

Export your movie

You can NOT post either a Windows Movie Maker Project file or an iMovie HD Project file to the Web, they are simply the working, editable versions of your movies. To create a postable movie file:

▶ **In Windows Movie Maker** Click "Save Movie File" under the "File" menu (not "Save Project") and choose your desired settings and file location. The medium quality "Web" option will give you the 320x240 resolution required (see tip).

▶ **In iMovie HD** Choose "QuickTime" from the "Share" menu and then select "Web Streaming" from the dropdown menu to get a resolution of 320x240 pixels. If you are feeling brave, you could try hitting "Expert Settings" and producing an MPEG-4 file (.mp4); mess around with the options to see the difference in picture quality and file size – you may well find it will give you better results.

When you are done, don't delete the original Project file, as you may want to tweak your edits or perhaps output the movie with different settings at a later date.

make it your own

output quality of your file and its onscreen size (or resolution). You can get by without knowing much, if any, of this, and just go with your software's default settings (see box on previous page), but it's good to experiment with what's on offer, if you want to squeeze the best possible picture and sound from your footage.

The process described in this chapter gives you pretty much the least you need to know about exporting files to be posted on MySpace Video. If you want to know more try online at: streaming.wisconsin.edu/creation/st_video.html

The upload process

To get your shiny new video clip up and running on MySpace Video, navigate to the "Video" homepage (there's a link for it on the main MySpace navigation bar) and click the "Upload Video" tab. Take note of the warning about uploading pornography, fill in a few details, check the box that says you agree to the MySpace "Terms and Conditions" and then click "Next".

Tip: If your movie clips are in any way personal think hard about whether you want to post them in such a public arena. At the very least during upload select the privacy option that prevents your movie from appearing in MySpace search results.

After choosing a couple of categories that best suit your clip and adding search tags (this is optional), browse for your file in exactly the same way you would if you were uploading images and music to MySpace. The file size upload limit is 100MB per movie, but bear in mind that the larger the file, the longer it will take to stream to its viewers, and long load times can frustrate anxious browsers into clicking away. While your upload finishes you are taken to your very own "My Videos" page, from where you can edit, delete and view your various uploaded movies.

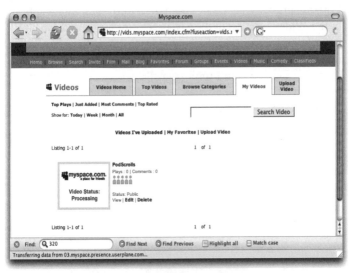

Note that after you upload, MySpace has to process the new file and convert it to the appropriate online "streaming" format, so don't expect to be able to view your file straight away.

Tip: You ceratinly don't have to host your clips with MySpace. They can reside on any Web space, or even with another video community such as YouTube.com. All you need to get them onto your Profile page is the appropriate code … read on.

Add video to your Profile pages

With the process that has just been described, your videos appear in the "Video" section of the MySpace community and can alternatively be reached via the "My videos" link below the default image on your Profile page. But it is also possible to embed video clips anywhere on your Profile page that you can paste the appropriate code (see p.128).

And we are not simply talking about your own video clips. Look on the page of any MySpace video clip and you will see, below the clip player, a series of links for adding a clip to your Profile, a blog or a bulletin. There is also a link to add a link to your "Favourites" list. Below that MySpace provides you with

Host your clips elsewhere

There are various sites and communities where you can post your video clips and generate links to their locations to use on your MySpace Profile. The largest is without a doubt YouTube (look for the "Embed" code below every clip), but there are loads more; some are simply free hosting services but others, like YouTube, offer a full community experience.

DropShots www.dropshots.com
Google video.google.com
Photobucket photobucket.com
TinyPic tinypic.com
YouTube www.youtube.com

All the sites listed above will, in one form or another, spit out the codes you need to embed your video clips on MySpace. If, however, you simply want to post your video files on some blog-standard Web space, perhaps provided by your ISP, you are going to have to build your own codes … gulp!

Not to worry, it really is pretty straightforward. The most important think is in include the information about the type of video file you want to stream; this will tell the browser of anyone looking for your clip exactly what it needs to do to display the file on-screen. Here are some example video codes for the most common video formats:

▶ **QuickTime Video:**
<embed src="http://www.yourserver.com/yourfile.mov"
type="video/quicktime" autostart="0" loop="0" height="240"
width="320"></embed>

▶ **Windows Media Video:**
<embed src="http://www.yourserver.com/yourfile.wmv"
type="application/x-mplayer2" autostart="0" loop="0" height="240"
width="320"></embed>

▶ **RealPlayer Video:**
<embed src="http://www.yourserver.com/yourfile.ram"
type="audio/x-pn-realaudio-plugin" autostart="0" loop="0" height="240"
width="320"></embed>

make it your own

Tip: If you find that pasting video codes into your Profile generates extraneous pieces of text on the previewed page, go back in to the code and edit the offending material out – it should not effect the link to the embedded video clip.

the URL of the video clip, if you want to direct someone to its location, and also the video code that you can use to embed the video clip on your own Profile. Simply select and copy (Ctrl+C or Apple+C) the code and then paste (Ctrl+V or Apple+V) it into whichever field you like on your "Edit Profile" page.

More video codes

As well as using links to clips that you have posted on non-MySpace websites, you can pilfer links to other people's video clips and add them to your Profile, blog, a bulletin, or even as part of comment on someone else's Profile page.

Many MySpacers use video code to decorate their Profile pages with pop promos by their favourite artist. Aside from the numerous codes that can be picked up within the MySpace community, there are many sites that specialize in providing video codes for all the top artists as well as a fair number of obscure ones. Expect to find a link or two back to the site included with the code, and you'll just have to put up with all the ads and pop-ups on these kind of sites. The following are little easier to deal with than many of the others:

Videos4u videocodes4u.com
VideoCodeZone www.videocodezone.com
Videosta www.videosta.com

Part 4

MySpace Music

18

Artist SignUp

building a band profile

Arguably the most captivating section of the entire MySpace site is MySpace Music – the home of thousands and thousands of solo artists, groups from every imaginable genre and even record labels. And the best thing about this gargantuan sonic ant's nest, is that nearly every single Profile page offers tracks for you to listen to, there and then, for free. It's the world's largest listening-post. Browsing the site's pages you will stumble upon everyone from the largest names within the music industry to kids who have belted out tracks in their bedroom, perhaps only minutes before you found and heard them. This chapter will show you how to become a part of the mix.

Musicians' FAQs

Do I need to be a musician to have a MySpace Music page?

You don't need to be in a "proper band" to set up a MySpace Music Profile; if you make music of any kind and you want to share your efforts with the world, go right ahead. For some pointers on how to record and mix your tracks see p.177.

My favourite band doesn't have a MySpace page ... can I set one up for them?

No ... there are legal implications in uploading material when you do not own the copyright. MySpace music pages are strictly there for you to make your music available, not other people's.

Will people download my music illegally?

Probably not. The only thing that's illegal is taking copyrighted material that you haven't acquired legitimately. While you're checking the small print, you will discover that when signing up as a musician

dkimages.com

with MySpace, any tracks you post are made freely available for other community members to download. Of course, if they then distribute your copyrighted material, they are breaking the law.

How do I make the right kind of file to upload my music?

You're talking about MP3s. And making them is a lot easier than you might think. It can, more than likely, be accomplished with software you already have on your computer. See p.179 for a guide to turning your recordings into MP3s.

Is it true that if I post my songs on my Profile page, MySpace own them?

There has been some heated debate on the subject of MySpace's user agreement, in which the wording of a clause implied that uploading music granted MySpace a "royalty free worldwide licence" to distribute the music. MySpace has stated it merely intends to share the music in the manner that the artist desires, and is working to modify the clause to clarify it. Of course, removing your music from the site nullifies any right MySpace has to do anything with it.

Can I sell my songs on MySpace?

At the time of writing, it was just announced that this will be possible in the future. There are millions of bands already showcasing their tunes on MySpace, so they were sure to make the move eventually. The interesting thing is that this development could

MySpace music

seriously threaten the iTunes Music Store's domination of the music download market, but only time will tell.

At present, it appears that MySpace will take a hefty percentage of all music sales, and they are looking at the possibility of working with PayPal (the online payment system owned by eBay) to get the process moving.

Sign up here...

Signing up as a band, or artist, on MySpace, is very much like signing up for a regular MySpace account (covered on p.60), though it has to be done from the "Artist SignUp" link on the music.myspace.com homepage, and some of the information you are required to provide will be a little different – "sounds like", "band members" etc. It's all very easy … even your drummer could do it.

Manage your Profile

Your Hello page as a MySpace Music artist is similar to a regular MySpacer's, though there are a few differences worth noting once you dig down into the settings pages.

Clicking on "Edit Profile" takes you to a tabbed form where you can fill in the following details:

Upcoming shows

Gigs added here are displayed on your profile. It's worth filling all of the fields in, including the venue address, otherwise your shows may not pop up when fans try to track down concerts in their area (see p.186). It's also important to set the correct "Country", otherwise the difference in timezones may cause your gig to disappear from the listings halfway though the day that it occurs. It's also worth following up gig listings with a well timed bulletin (see p.109).

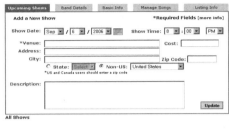

Tip: This form also features a list of all your previous show listings, which you can edit or delete at any time.

Band details

This is similar to the "Interests and Personality" section of a regular MySpace page, with the categories geared more towards bands – instead of "About Me", for example, you have "Bio" and instead of "Music" you have "Influences".

Also the interface is slightly different, rather than entering information directly into a form you have to click a link to edit each category individually. The field marked "Website" provides somewhere to stick an external link to your band or label's site. There's no need to use any HTML code here, just type the web address and it'll make the link automatically.

Basic info

Just what it says on the tin – basic information about your location and band's name (which is used as the "Display Name" at the head of your Profile page and in other people's Friends lists).

Listing info

Here you can pick up to three genres that best describe your music from a fair, but less than exhaustive list. You first have to hit the "Edit" button beneath the form to unlock the drop-down menus. You can also change your band's MySpace URL from this page – something you can't do with a regular MySpace profile.

Manage your songs

Once you have your songs in MP3 format and under 6MB in size (see p.179), this is where you'll upload them. You're currently allowed to add 4 songs in total, though this is likely to change when MySpace makes download sales a reality.

On this page there are also some tick boxes that'll allow you to specify basic settings for your uploaded tracks – whether or not to allow users to add a song to their profile, whether to make a song auto-play when the profile is viewed, and whether multiple songs should be played randomly or in sequence.

Clicking on the "Add a Song" link takes you to a page where you enter details about the track you want to upload. It also pro-

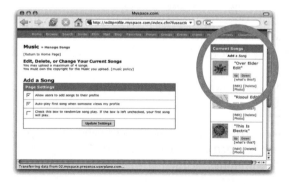

vides a field for you to type or paste the lyrics (a link to the lyrics will appear under the song title in the MySpace MP3 player on your Profile page) and a box to check or uncheck depending on whether you want people to be able to "rank" your efforts by scoring them out of ten.

Tip: This is also the place where you get to choose whether your tracks are "downloadable"; do you want people to simply stream the music from your Profile page, or be able to download their own copy of the MP3 to listen to whenever they want.

When you're ready, click "Update" and then browse for file on your computer and upload it. You'll then have to wait for a short time while your song uploads. You might also get a warning about uploading music that does not belong to you. If you are at all unsure about copyright and how it relates to you, find out as soon as you can – even if you know you have not infringed on anyone else's copyright, you should think about protecting your own tunes (see box overleaf).

Next you'll be prompted to upload an image to accompany your song. This could be an album cover or anything else you'd like, and will appear in the small window to the left of the song list in the MySpace MP3 player. You'll find that this is one of the only instances where MySpace actually re-sizes and optimizes the image to fit in a space – it still won't accept massive files, however, so it's worth referring to the section on image optimization (see

Safe mode

You get into safe mode by clicking a text link just next to your Edit Profile link on your Hello Page. Once in Safe Mode you can edit code into or out of your Profle info, Groups, Comments and Image Captions – useful for removing dead links from people's comments while keeping the comment itself intact. For more information on editing HTML code see p.125.

p.151) for tips on how to get your file at least in the ballpark of an appropriate size.

Once your image is uploaded you'll be informed that the song is being converted to MySpace's streaming format and will be available within 24 hours. Your track then appears in the "Current Songs" panel, accompanied by the word "Processing" until it has been successfully converted.

You can go back at any time and edit your songs' details, change their images, delete them altogether or change the order that they appear in the MP player.

Copyright

Music copyright is a great big can of worms. There are all sorts of issues you may want to consider, such as whether or not any samples on your recordings require permissions for use. You may also want to protect your own mechanical and performance rights to the music you've written. For detailed information you can contact the MCPS-PRS Alliance in the UK and the ASCAP in the US.

MCPS-PRS www.mcps-prs-alliance.co.uk/aboutcopyright
ASCAP www.ascap.com

19

Making music

get the most out of your recordings

Before getting as far as uploading songs to MySpace, you're going to need to find a way to record and mix your music and get it into the right file format. Obviously the sky's the limit as far as music production expertise, equipment and costs go. But fear not, it's amazing what you can do without shelling out a fortune on gear, and there's plenty of free editing software to be found online. What's more, you don't need a degree in studio engineering to create the sound you want. The next few pages offer enough pointers to get you started.

Record your music

You may already have recordings that you want to post on MySpace – perhaps recorded to 4-track tape or straight onto your computer. If you're just starting out, however, the cheapest option is to snare some free recording and sound editing software such as GarageBand (which has shipped with all new Macs sold in the last few years, see www.apple.com/ilife) or, for PC users, the share-ware applications Reaper (www.reaper.fm) or Audacity (audacity.sourceforge.net). Whether you're looking to record multiple tracks to your computer or simply work on a stereo track for mastering purposes, these programs should give you what you need. For a couple more commercial options, see p.36.

Master for MySpace

Mastering is the process where the finished mix of your song is treated as a single stereo recording (as opposed to separate channels for each instrument) and processed in order to smooth out differences between songs – for example, on an album where EQ and volume levels need to be consistent. For the purposes of both recording and mastering you'll probably be working with WAV

> **Tip:** When mixing or mastering, take regular breaks away from listening and come back with fresh ears. Standing further back in the room will give you a better idea about what's going on in the lower register. You can also try standing outside the room and listening to your mix; it'll give you a clue as to whether anything is too loud or quiet. Once you think it's in the bag, burn your finished recording onto a CD and try it out in different rooms, at friends' houses, or even in the car.

or AIFF files. This are uncompressed audio formats that take up a lot of space, and as such totally unsuitable for uploading to the Web.

When setting the EQ for a mix it's best to listen to tracks in a variety of environments and on a number of different speakers. Some people will listen to your songs through tiny PC or laptop speakers, while others will have their computers wired up to a Hi-Fi. Ideally, you should be able to switch between a decent pair of speakers that you know and trust, and a smaller pair of computer speakers. Try to keep the EQ on your amplifier "flat" and get used to listening to music at this setting. This will deliver a more objective representation of your sound and you won't be fooled into overcompensating for too much bass, not enough treble, and so on.

Ultimately, your music will be heard on a broad spectrum of systems so try to keep your EQ fairly conservative (listening to similar music with your amp's EQ flat for reference).

Once you're happy with a track you'll need to convert the uncompressed WAV or AIFF file into a compressed MP3 format in order to upload it to MySpace.

Make your MP3

MySpace currently limits file size for uploaded songs to 6MB, for a 3-minute song this should be more than adequate to get a great-sounding MP3, anything larger and you enter into the grey area of file size versus sound quality. But don't panic; it's still possible to get a decent sound with heavier compression settings, so you may be able to share that rock opera with the world after all.

There are many programs that'll make your music into MP3s, the most obvious being iTunes (www.apple.com/itunes), which

Why MP3s?

Music on computers can be stored in numerous file formats, but the main one you need to know about is the ubiquitous MP3 (or Moving Pictures Experts Group-1/2 Audio Layer 3 to give it its rather grandiose full title). Like JPEGs (see p.150) for images, this format is designed for squeezing lots of information into a very small files; in fact, technically speaking, the name MP3 refer not just to the file format but also to the "compression algorithms" used to do the squeezing. When a computer turns an uncompressed audio file into an MP3, the resulting file sounds almost identical to the original but is around ninety percent smaller. That means ten times quicker downloads from the Internet. This compression is achieved through a remarkable combination of mathematics and psychoacoustics: the algorithms are clever enough to take out what your brain does not process (the vast majority of the sound) and leave the rest untouched. For a full explanation, see: www.mp3-converter.com/mp3codec

is free for Mac or PC, or you may find that your sound editing sofware has a function for saving files directly as MP3s. A good list of MP3 encoders can be found here: www.mp3-converter.com

iTunes conversions

Some of the software already mentioned in this chapter will allow you to output your finished songs as MP3s, though you might find it far easier to do the job in Apple's free iTunes program (which you probably already have). Aside from being a generally very intuitive application, its MP3 conversions tools allow all the flexibility you need to try out a song at various bitrates.

Whether you are using the program on a PC or a Mac, the process is the

> **Tip:** If you want to try out various different MP3 bitrates, always convert from the original uncompressed version, rather than one of your other freshly minted MP3s.

same. Import your uncompressed track into iTunes. Then specify the MP3 format and bitrate under "Importing" options (within iTunes Preferences, under the "Advanced" tab). Then select the file in question and choose "Convert selection to MP3" from the "Advanced" or right-click menus.

iTunes www.apple.com/itunes

Which bitrate?

The bitrate of an MP3 is the amount of data that each second of sound is reduced to. The higher the bitrate, the higher the sound

LAME MP3 encoding

There's more than one way to skin a cat, and there's more than one way to encode an MP3 file. The encoder built into iTunes does a decent-enough job, but there are alternatives out there that arguably do it better. Indeed, there's a near-consensus among people who are interested in such things that the best MP3 encoder for files with a bitrate of 128 Kbps or higher is the open-source (non-copyrighted) software known as LAME. (Its somewhat self-deprecating name stands, bizarrely enough, for "LAME Ain't an MP3 Encoder".)

Mac users who fancy getting the audiophile benefits of LAME can grab the easy-to-use iTunes-LAME script (www.blacktree.com/apps/iTunes-LAME), which adds LAME encoding to iTunes via the Scripts menu. Once installed, you can use LAME when importing tracks from a CD, and also when converting songs into MP3 from other formats. If you have a PC, you'll find various free programs featuring LAME encoding at lame.sourceforge.net/links.html

Tip: Frequencies below 10Hz are inaudible to humans, so removing them should reduce the size of your files without affecting the sound. But try a test file, as some audiophiles have commented that removing these frequencies can result in an unbalanced sound and even a tinnitus-like ringing in the recording.

quality, but also the more disk space the track takes up. The relationship between file size and bitrate is basically proportional, but the same isn't true of sound quality, so a 128 Kbps track takes half as much space as the same track recorded at 256 Kbps, but the sound will be only very marginally different.

Another option is to use Variable Bit Rate, or VBR, which adjusts the bitrate in real time, according to the complexity of the sound. With some music, this can save quite a lot of disk space. The best approach is to start at 192 Kbps and if the file is too big, work your way down through lower bitrate and VBR settings until your file is under 6MB. Once your music gets converted into MySpace's streaming format it's going to sound a bit swooshy in the top end anyway, so rolling off higher frequencies and encoding at a lower bitrate may translate better than you'd think. Experiment and find out what works best with your material.

20 More music

the MySpace music page

So, you've got your songs up and running, your profile is all set and everything works, what now? Do you want to add videos? Spread the word about your band? Do you fancy worming your way onto the MySpace Music homepage? This chapter will show you everything else that MySpace can do for you and your music.

MySpace music

MySpace's music home page is accessible by clicking the "Music" link on the main MySpace navigation bar at the top of the screen. A new deep red bar appears, which contains links to the relevant music sections of the site (see opposite).

The bulk of the screen is taken up with items such as "Featured Artists" (basically just big flashy links to artists' MySpace pages, see p.188), a search facility, "Exclusives" (which tend to be some corporate tie-in), "Featured Video", "On Tour", and other stuff that you can pretty much ignore. There's also a "Top Genre" list – the way in for anyone browsing bands who choose to affiliate themselves with a particular sound. You may discover that much of the time bands deliberately pick genres to describe themselves for ironic humour points rather than descriptive usefulness, so if you're after the darkest death metal, for example, it may be worth augmenting your search to include bands under the "Christian

Rap" genre. Equally, some bands might well view themselves as "Experimental" within their particular field – whether it be hip-hop, reggae or rap – and add the tag to their Profile, making the genre a hodgepodge of every kind of remotely left-field music under the sun.

Music navigation bar

Music videos

The Music Videos section exists separately from MySpace Video (see p.157) and consists of musicians' videos (as opposed to fans' live footage, for example). It's searchable by band name or song name and/or genre. Selected videos open in a slightly ugly media-player style pop-up window with options for full screen mode, video quality, etc. At the time of writing this feature is still in development and may not even appear if you are using a Mac or non-Explorer browser.

Directory

This is an alphabetical list of all the musicians on MySpace. You can browse or search (narrowing by genre if you so desire). Not the most useful page in the world, but good to know it's there.

Search

A far more comprehensive and useful facility is offered behind the "Search" link – here you can define your search by genre, location, key words, etc, and sort the results by number of times played, number of friends, alphabetically, etc.

Top artists

The Top Artist page (not to be confused with MySpace's Featured Artists) is split into three categories – "Unsigned", "Indie", and "Major" – ranked by how many times their songs have been played that day.

Shows

This is a useful page where you can type a postcode (it defaults to your own postcode) and find out who's playing live within your area. Clicking on a band's name will take you to their page, and clicking on the venue name will take you to the venue's address and any other relevant information about the show. It also provides a link to add the event to your calendar.

Music forums

MySpace's forums are crawling with activity. The music forums are broken down into ten or so categories, such as acoustic, emo, hip-hop and so on. For more on forums see p.103.

Classifieds

The music classifieds page, by default, displays classified ad listings for Los Angeles. Clicking the "Change city" tab gives you a handful of options that will redirect you to the main classified area for your chosen location. From there you'll need to navigate your way into the music section.

Getting noticed

There are a stack of things you can do to increase your profile as a band on MySpace. Given that most people stumble across new tunes by flitting from one Friends list to another, it's worthwhile making friends (see p.83) with as many like-minded musicians as you can. Don't go crazy though, as many MySpacers who come face to face with a Friends list featuring thousands of names may well be put off by the volume. Here are a few other weapons at your disposal:

▶ Tell friends to add your songs to their Profile page by using the "Add" links on your Profile's MP3 Player (see p.137).

▶ Post regular bulletins (see p.109) and keep your shows list updated. If people don't know you have a show … they won't go.

▶ Change your pictures and songs often … it will encourage people to come back regularly to see what's new.

MySpace music

▶ Post "flyers" for your gigs as image comments (see p.98) on the Profile page of everyone in your Friends list, or at the very least, everyone who lives in the vicinity of the show and are likely to turn up. For a great online flyer-building tool, check out:

Band Flyers
www.band-flyers.com

Featured Artists

Finally, a word on Featured Artists. These are musicians that MySpace has chosen to endorse for one reason or another. They have their pictures posted on the MySpace music front page that link to the bands' profiles. If you'd like to try your luck at becoming a Featured Artist go to the MySpace FAQs page (there's a link at the bottom of every MySpace page) and select the first question in the list. You'll be taken to a form for sending a Featured Artist request to customer services, after which a representative will contact you … good luck.

Part 5

Playing it safe

21

Avoiding trouble

socializing safely in MySpace and other online communities

Despite some nasty stories that have made headlines and raised alarms, online communities do not represent the end of civilization as we know it. Yes, there are dangers (see p.38), but the most prevalent of them are ignorance and fear. Parents need to see that online communities can be a positive thing, while teens need to treat them with the caution and respect that they warrant. To give you a bit of perspective, you wouldn't step into the road with your eyes closed. Read on for a description of the most important steps to take to stay safe on MySpace and other online communities.

Privacy and security

Both MySpace and many of the other online communities offer a number of tools and settings to help members maintain some degree of privacy while online.

On MySpace, all of these settings are found within "Account Settings", which is linked to from your Hello page. From the "Account Settings" page explore "Privacy Settings" (pictured below), but also take the time to examine the additional privacy options hidden behind the other links on the page.

Private accounts

At the bottom of the "Privacy Settings" panel are options for determining whether you want your Profile to be private (only viewable by your friends, see box) or public (viewable by everyone, both MySpace members and non-MySpace members). If you are 14 or 15 years old, your account is automatically set to private, and you won't have the option of changing the setting until you turn 16.

With a private Profile, you can still

Privacy Settings	
☑	Require email or last name to add me as a friend
☐	Approve Comments before Posting
☐	Hide Online Now
☑	Show My Birthday to my Friends 🍗
☐	No Pic Forwarding
☐	Friend Only Blog Comments
☐	Block Friend Request From Bands
☐	Friend Only Group Invites
Who Can View My Full Profile	
○	My Friends Only
◉	Public
Change Settings	**Cancel**

Know your friends

MySpace privacy settings have an obvious purpose, but their success largely depends on the people in your Friends list actually being your friends – that is to say, people you can trust. Of course, in the majority of cases this will be true, especially if you choose to maintain a network of friends drawn from people you know in the real world, perhaps through school or college.

However, when MySpacers strive to create Friends lists large enough to populate a small continent, the notion that a Friends list can, in any meaningful sense, be a "private" network, goes out the window.

Even MySpacers with a network of thousands probably only communicate regularly with enough friends to fill a school bus.

dkimages.com

More worrying are the few instances of adults creating bogus MySpace accounts for the purpose of connecting with, and gaining the confidence of, younger teenagers (see p.38). Obviously, maintaining a private account helps, but you can still receive Friends Requests and unwittingly approve someone who may well be highly dubious.

The answer to this problem is to be cautious. Understand the implications of making someone your MySpace friend and, most importantly, the freedom this gives them to communicate with you and to add comments to your Profile page.

And remember, if someone on your Friends list gives you any trouble, or leads you to suspect they are not who they say they are, they can always be removed from your list (see p.90) or blocked altogether (see p.204).

receive Friends Requests (see p.86) and your details will still be searchable (see p.71), but only people in your Friends list will be able to see your Profile page, photos, Friends list, etc. This is a great option for teenagers who want to network and socialize within a small group that mirrors their circle of school friends. However, a Private account is only as private as you make it; if you are in the habit of asking every Tom, Dick and Harry whose profile you encounter to be your friend, then you are rather missing the point of the excercise.

The privacy flipside

There is, however, a negative aspect to Private accounts. They can be used to foster small, insular groups, among both teenagers and adults, where less-than-desirable subjects can be discussed or obscene material posted, without any scrutiny or safeguards.

> **Tip for parents:** If you have younger teenagers using Private accounts on MySpace, talk to them about the idea of setting up a MySpace account yourself and becoming their "friend". You could then come to an agreement about not logging in and checking up on them without their consent. This should provide you with peace of mind, while also allowing your teenagers to maintain control of their own online experience.

Stay private

As well as all the concerns that are frequently raised about paedophiles, grooming (see p.38) and the dangers of encounters with strangers, it is important to realize that whatever you write or post on your online community Profile page can leave you open to attack from sources much closer to home. Every school or college, without exception, contains a certain number of numbskulls looking to bully, pester or embarrass their classmates; for this reason there is much to be said for maintaining a low profile online. Here are a number of MySpace measures that can help make your social networking experience as hassle-free as possible:

▶ Don't let people see whether or not you are online. This option is to be found in the "Privacy Settings" panel.

▶ Don't post compromising material. This is likely to make you an instant target for ridicule or abuse.

▶ Don't post personal details. On p.71, this book describes the kind of information that MySpace allows you to add to your Profile. Think carefully about what you divulge and how anything you say could be used against you.

▶ Approve other people's comments before they are posted. This option is to be found within the "Privacy Settings" panel and will allow you to vet all comments added to your Profile before they reach public scrutiny. If you do not enable this screening function, be sure to visit your Profile page regularly to check for unwanted material, and delete it straight away (see p.97).

▶ Don't allow picture forwarding. By default, MySpace will allow someone looking at your "My Pictures" page to forward the images to any email address. To disable this function, check the "No Pic Forwarding" radio button in the "Privacy Settings" panel.

▶ Only allow Group invites from friends – another setting found under "Privacy Settings". This is especially useful if you find yourself bombarded with invitations to join "junk" MySpace Groups.

Maintain security

Just as important as privacy is the security of your account details. Here are a few golden rules that should stop anyone else logging on as you or stealing your personal login details:

▶ Create an unguessable password (see p.63) and change it regularly using the link on the "Account Settings" page.

▶ Never share your password with anyone. Even best friends.

▶ Always log out at the end of your session (see p.74).

▶ Don't let friends "have a quick go" on MySpace while your account is logged in – you never know what damage they could end up doing in your name.

▶ Never set a computer to remember your login details.

▶ Don't log in unless you know the page you see is part of MySpace. This should stop you being snared by phishing scams (see p.43). To be sure, look at the address bar of your browser to check that the displayed domain name is correct. You should either see http://login.myspace.com/... if you are looking at the MySpace login page (pictured) or http://www.myspace.com if you are on the MySpace homepage.

It is also worth remembering that MySpace is not immune from viruses and fraudsters. With this in mind:

▶ Never give out your credit card or personal details. MySpace is not a secure environment for passing on any kind of payment details in exchange for a product or service.

▶ Never agree to pay for any MySpace codes on MySpace, or on any other website for that matter. If you do feel compelled to "contribute" a small donation to an independent software developer, only do so using a recognized online payment system such as PayPal. Find out more at: www.paypal.com

▶ When browsing MySpace code or tweak sites, including any listed in this book, do not accept downloads for "browser enhancements" or applications unless you are completely sure what they are.

▶ Protect your computer and operating system from viruses and online attacks (see p.32).

> **Tip:** For more of the general dos and don'ts of online security, pick up a copy of *The Rough Guide To The Internet*.

Real-world encounters

The reactionary answer to the question of whether or not you should meet up with people you've communicated with online is, "just don't do it". However, there are always going to be grey areas. While going to the concert of a band you have befriended on MySpace will probably lead to a headache at worst, arranging a private rendezvous for social, romantic or sexual reasons could result in something rather worse.

playing it safe

If you really must meet up with an individual you have only ever communicated with online (or by phone), then you should always follow these rules:

▶ Meet somewhere public and well populated, such as a café or shopping mall, and preferably in a place you already know.

▶ Take at least one friend with you; even better, invite the person to hang out with you and a whole crowd of your friends, rather than agreeing to a "date" or a one-to-one situation.

▶ Make sure a responsible person knows where you are going, who you are going with, and at what time you are going to be back.

▶ Do not get into a car with the person or agree to go anywhere with them other than where you have already arranged.

▶ Prearrange your own journey home, and do not accept any offers to be taken home or walked home.

▶ Do not give out your home address.

Be realistic

However well you think you know someone through chatting to them online … you don't. They are still strangers with unknown intentions. Don't be fooled by even the most heart-melting promise of love or affection. It sounds harsh, but it really is better to be safe than sorry. And even if the person you are meeting is a fellow teenager, any encounter (sexual or otherwise) is potentially dangerous. For more advice, visit:

Safeteens.com www.safeteens.com

22

Dealing with difficulties

where to find help

With any luck you should never have to read this chapter, and if you follow the safety advice scattered throughout this book you stand an excellent chance of avoiding the worst problems associated with MySpace and other online communities. The most important thing is to know who to turn to if something goes wrong – keeping difficulties to yourself will only make things worse.

Identity theft

Identity theft is a serious problem, and can take two forms. Either an individual creates a false account and pretends to be someone else, or, by managing to get hold of someone else's login details, they take control of their account and play havoc with the existing content, or post offensive comments to other people's Profiles in the victim's name.

Someone is using your account...

If you ever come to your Profile page and realize that some of your content seems to have changed (see box opposite), or you

Deal with bad code

Though discovering your page in disarray might lead you to believe that
someone has logged in using your password, it might also be the case that
some bad HTML code is causing the problem. Perhaps it was even you that
entered the code; in which case you will need to check your "Edit Profile"
page for any problems, or you might try removing the last piece of code you
added. If, however, you believe the problem stems from some code added
by someone else in the form of a comment, remove the comment (see p.97),
or edit it using "Safe Mode" (see p.97).

find out that someone is posting comments in your name, change
your password straight away, using the link in the "Account
Settings" panel.

Of course, whoever has stolen your login details may have
already changed your password, in which case you won't even
be able to log in to MySpace. In this case, use the "Forgot Your
Password?" link just below the login fields to reach a form
(pictured opposite) from which you can retrieve your account's
current password and have it sent to the email address that you
originally signed-up with.

If, for whatever reason, this does not work, and you still cannot get access to your account, contact MySpace using the form
described on p.202 and send the MySpace administrators a
"salute" (also explained in more detail on p.202).

In the majority of such cases, victims will have a good idea who
the culprit is; if this is the case, talk to a parent or teacher rather
than confronting them yourself. It will also be worth trying to
minimize any damage that has been done by telling everyone on
your Friends list what has happened and asking them to remove
any offending comments (see p.97) posted on their Profile pages
under your name during the period in question.

Someone has created a fake Profile in your name...

In this situation, MySpace requires you to verify your identity by sending them the Web address of the false Profile page and a "salute". In their words, this salute is "an image of yourself holding a handwritten sign with the word 'MySpace.com' and your Friend ID". This ID number can be found in the address bar of your Web browser when viewing your genuine Profile page. If you don't actually have a MySpace Profile, include your email address instead of your Friend ID.

This is all done by contacting MySpace's customer services department using the "Contact MySpace" link at the bottom of the MySpace homepage. From the two dropdown menus, select "Reporting Abuse" and "Identity theft" as the subjects of your message. The MySpace authorities will then remove the false

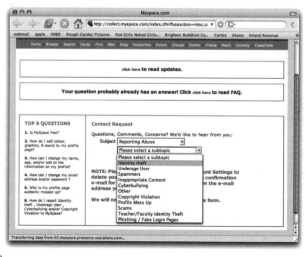

Technical problems

The form pictured opposite can also be used to contact MySpace regarding any technical problems you may encounter with your MySpace Profile, or any error messages from across the site as a whole. Given the size of the community, and the amount of data and traffic that MySpace has to deal with each day, it is inevitable that there will be the occasional problem with servers, power failures and the like.

To avoid sending a message that highlights a problem they're already aware of, click the "read updates" link at the top of the "Contact MySpace" form to see what issues are currently being dealt with.

Tip: You can also find numerous links for contacting MySpace about all the issues discussed in this chapter within the various MySpace FAQ pages. These include a specific link for teachers who have had false Profile pages created in their name. The FAQs pages can be reached from the link at the bottom of the MySpace homepage.

Profile from the site. Again, some kind of damage-limitation exercise is a good idea to ensure that none of your friends have been fooled by the offending Profile page.

Bullying and harassment

This topic covers a range of problems, from your peers simply trying to get a rise out of you to far more serious episodes of bullying and abuse. Whatever the form of the harassment, the most important thing is to not overreact. Just ignore inflammatory messages and comments that come your way, and then take steps (see below) to prevent the bully from making contact with you again. In most instances, once ignored, a bully will soon get bored and go away. There are numerous things you can do to combat these kinds of attacks:

▶ Tell someone what's happening. It doesn't have to be a parent, but it should be someone you trust.

▶ Don't reply to any messages that you have been sent via the MySpace messaging system. If you want, delete the messages without reading them, though it can also be a good idea to keep hold of such messages so that you can prove what has been going on at a later date, if necessary.

▶ Delete any comments that the bully has left on your Profile page, but again, copy and paste their contents somewhere else in case you ever need a document of the abuse. Then, using the option within "Privacy Settings", set your account so that you have to approve all comments before they're posted.

▶ Remove the person from your Friends list so that they will no longer be able to add comments to your Profile page.

▶ Block the user who is causing you trouble by viewing their Profile page and clicking the "Block User" link in their "Contacting…" panel; this will stop them from contacting you.

▶ If the bully is also bad-mouthing you to other people in your network of friends, ask your friends to delete those comments and to block the person in question as well.

Tip: For more safety tips and advice, look online. MySpace has several pages of advice buried within the FAQs pages, while this book also lists several websites in its Resources chapter (see p.215).

▶ Contact the MySpace customer services department (see p.202) and send them the Friend ID (see p.45) of the bully, as well as the details of your own account.

> **Tip:** The form reached via the "Contact MySpace" link on the website's homepage can also be used for reporting most other MySpace related problems, from copyright infringements to fake login pages and spammers.

Serious threats

In the case of any serious threats to either your personal safety or your property, get in touch with your local police or law enforcement agency immediately.

Reporting inappropriate material

Due to the size of MySpace, which now comprises millions of pages and users, and the fact that there are no real checks or balances on what is posted on those pages, it is very important that MySpace members report inappropriate material whenever it is encountered.

For a full list of what is deemed to be undesirable, read the "Terms" page of the site, reached via the link at the bottom of the MySpace homepage. In brief, the kind of material that we are talking about includes anything that promotes racism, bigotry or hatred; anything that contains nudity, violence, offensive subject matter or contains a link to "adult" websites; anything that promotes illegal activities or anything defamatory or libellous. The list of prohibited material goes on, and also touches upon copyright infringements, spam and the posting of individual's images without their consent.

All of this material should be reported to MySpace using the "Contact MySpace" form already described, but you can also easily report individual offensive images from any user's "View my Pics" page by clicking the "Report This Image" link below the offending picture.

MySpace addiction

Finally, a word on MySpace addiction. Various reports in the media have suggested that many teenagers are becoming far too reliant on the website and their online groups of friends. The argument claims that MySpacers have such immediate access to an arena of interaction and social engagement that they are losing their capacity for self-reliance, even forgetting how to be "bored" – arguably an important component of emotional and imaginative development.

Whether or not you hold sway with such notions, on a purely practical level, spending too much time online is going to interfere with your studies, real-world relationships and the like. If you think you, or someone you know, is developing a MySpace addiction, look for help online at:

WikiHow www.wikihow.com/Defeat-a-MySpace-Addiction

And to share your pain, or read what others have to say, visit: www.43things.com/things/view/5970

Part 6

MySpaceology

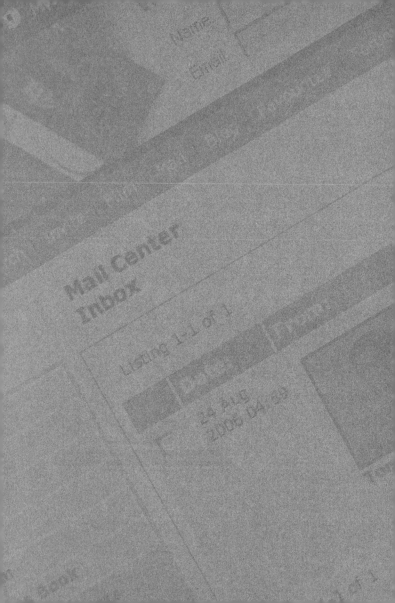

23
MySpace weirdness

stranger than fiction

I t goes without saying that MySpace cradles some pretty crazy stuff – all you need to sign up is an email address, so what is there to stop you from setting yourself up online as a tree, banana, pancake, toilet brush or chair? Nothing! Read on…

Member Login

E-Mail:

Password:

☐ Remember Me

LOGIN   SIGN UP!

Forgot your password?

Display name: Butter

"I can't believe... oh wait... it is me!!!"

Yes, everyone's favourite dairy product has made a home for itself on MySpace. This tasty addition to your friends list includes "being churned" and "being whipped" among his many interests and counts among his numerous friends, "lard", "toast", "waffles" and "the potato".

Worst of MySpace

A great little site for those days when MySpace makes you want to throw your computer out of the window. There are rants about MySpace clichés, loads of links to the worst and weirdest Profile pages, and a very useful guide entitled "How to not suck at MySpace".

Worst Of MySpace
www.worstofmyspace.com
www.myspace.com/worstof

Worst MySpace personalities

This article presents a quick run-through of the ten most hated types of people on MySpace, from the "Self-Righteous Emo Kid" to the "No Shirt Guy" and, umm, "Tom". Drop by and hope that none of the hats fit.

Blogcritics.org
blogcritics.org/archives/2006
/01/11/055249.php

MySpaceology

Display name: Chair

"Would you like to sit down?"

Considering how much of his time is spent staring at people's backsides, this particular item of furniture turns out to be a very jolly, amenable sort of fellow. On the subject of films, Chair says: "My favourite movie is *Fight Club*. My brother was in it, you know! Edward Norton sat on him in one of the self-help seminar scenes! He's a celebrity where I come from, really."

MySpace haircuts

You don't need a website to tell you that MySpace offers a delectable smorgasbord of crimps, cuts and hirsute hilarity … but here's a couple anyway.

The First Annual MySpace Stupid Haircut Awards
www.demonbaby.com/blog/2004/04/first-annual-myspace-stupid-haircut.html

The Second Annual MySpace Stupid Haircut Awards
www.demonbaby.com/blog/2006/01/second-annual-myspace-stupid-haircut.html

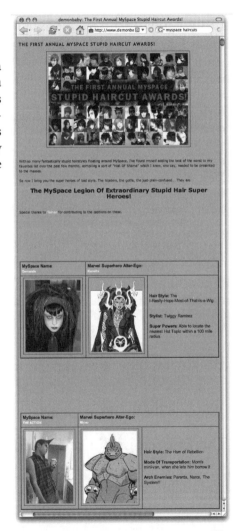

Only on MySpace...

Along with pretty much anything else you can think of, toys are well represented on MySpace. You can find everything from Barbies and My Little Ponies to this rather rad Lego Star Wars Snowtrooper:

www.myspace.com/ legosnowtrooper

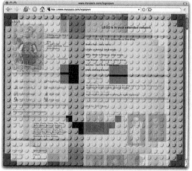

And while we are on a Lego tip, for easily the best background image on the planet, pay a visit to: www.myspace.com/ legospwn

The Encyclopedia of Stupid

And finally, the MySpace entry on the wonderful Encyclopedia of Stupid is worth a gander:

www.encyclopediaofstupid.com/stupid/index.php/Myspace

24
MySpace resources

websites & blogs

I f you want to find out more about any of the subjects covered in this book – or track down that chimeric piece of Profile page code – you're going to have to hit the Web. There's an almost frightening number of MySpace-related sites out there, including comprehensive code sites and various online safety portals. The MySpace site itself is a useful resource (their FAQs page is as good a place as any to start), and there are even blogs devoted to the topic of online communities. The following are the pick of the bunch (but for a glance at some of the weirder MySpace finds, turn to p.209).

Layout generators and hack sites

It has been said at numerous points throughout this book, but is still worth reiterating: stay alert when browsing these code sites and only use them to harvest codes – never accept to download any applications or plug-ins. For more on MySpace codes and hacks, see p.121.

DooBix.com www.doobix.com
FreeCodeSource.com www.freecodesource.com
GameSpot www.gamespot.com
MySpacePimper.com www.myspacepimper.com

MySpace Updates myspaceupdates.com
Pimp-My-Profile.com www.pimp-my-profile.com
PimpMySpace.org www.pimpmyspace.org
PureLayouts.com www.purelayouts.com
Skize.com www.skize.com
Strikefile www.strikefile.com/myspace
YourCoolProfile.com www.yourcoolprofile.com

MySpaceology

Safety tips

There are loads of great Internet safety sites to be found online by Googling; most offer good advice, though some tend to dish it up in a rather alarmist tone. Try these sites first:

BlogSafety.com www.blogsafety.com
CommonSense
www.myspace.com/CommonSenseMedia & www.commonsense.com
CyberTipline www.cybertipline.com
NetSmartz www.netsmartz.org
Staysafe.org www.staysafe.org
Web Wise Kids www.wiredwithwisdom.org

Though many of the resources listed opposite are useful for both teens and parents, here are a few more aimed at the grown-ups:

Parents Guide to MySpace www.parentsguidetomyspace.com
Social Shield socialshield.com
Wired Safety www.wiredsafety.org/internet101/myspaceguide.html

And for advice from the US federal government:

OnguardOnline onguardonline.gov/socialnetworking_youth.html

MySpace blogs

It can seem like an impossible task to sift through all the MySpace blogs (see p.111) to find something interesting, so here's a link that should help you home in on the good stuff:

SpaceCadetz www.spacecadetz.com

To see what's been freshly posted on MySpace blogs, visit Technorati for its indexed links to the most recent (although not necessarily the most interesting) blog entries:

Technorati www.technorati.com/tags/myspace

And more...

For an overview of what social networking is all about and how MySpace has changed over the years, visit the relevant pages of Wikipedia, starting with:

Wikipedia en.wikipedia.org/wiki/Myspace

Index

Index

a

About Me 71, 130
Account Settings 73, 137
addiction to MySpace 206
address book 93
adds 84, 89
aggregator 113
AIFF file 179
alumni 81
AmphetaDesk 113
Anderson, Tom 54
animated GIFs 151
anonymity 72
Apple 32, 82
approve comments 97
Artist SignUp 169
ASCAP 176
AsianAvenue 54
Audacity 36, 178
audio comments 145
Auqio Sound Studio 36
avatars 20

b

Background & Lifestyle 72
background images 136
background music 137
badge creator 18

Band Details 173

Band Details 173
band-flyers.com 188
banner ads 140
Basic Info 72, 173
bass (EQ) 179
Bebo 7, 15, 125, 134, 147
bitrates 181
BlackPlanet 54
block…
    comments 96
    user 204
Blog Control Center 114
Blog Groups 112
blogging 17, 111, 113
Bloglines 113
BlogSafety.com 218
Books, MySpace 119
broadband 27
browsing 77, 82
bulletins 106, 109
bullying 203

c

Calendars, MySpace 110
Campus Life 81
cancelling your account 76
Cascading Style Sheet 124, 131
Catster 24
celebrity friends 84
censoring tools 41

change…
    Account Settings 73
    password 63, 73
    Top Friends 89
Chat 99
    moderators 101
Chat rooms 101
Ciao.com 6
Circle of Friends 7, 8
Classifieds, MySpace 187
Classmates.com 6, 7, 19
closed communities 18
Club Penguin 24
code 72, 97, 124, 146, 201, 216
code generators 90, 216
Color Detector 126
colour codes 126
colour names 129
Comedy, MySpace 120
comments 95, 195
Communities, MySpace 117
compression 152, 180
contact MySpace 202
Contact… box 140
copyright 148, 170, 176, 206
CorelDraw 148
counters 138
create…
    account 60
    event 108
    group 105
CSS 124, 131
cursors 143
cyber bullying *see bullying*
cyber cafés 28

dangers 37, 38, 39, 56
Dashboard 82
death metal 126
delete…
    bulletins 109
    friends 90
    picture comment 98
    Profile comment 97
    your account 76
DeWolfe, Chris 54
dial-up 26
digital cameras 148, 158
digital video cameras 148, 158
DigitalColor Meter 126
Disable…
    HTML comments 96
    songs from automatically
    starting 80
discussion boards 106
Display Name 68, 71, 72
dithering images 126
Dogster 24
Dooyoo 6
downloading music 170
drawing software 148
DropShots 165
DV camcorders 148, 158
DVDs 159

eBay 21
editing…
    comments 97
    friends 90
    Profile 68, 172
email 11, 29
    accounts 11
    address 63
    free accounts 31
Encyclopedia of Stupid 214
Enemyster 16
Epinions 6
EQ 178
error messages 203
etiquette 102, 103

eUniverse 54
Events, MySpace 108
EverQuest 23

f

Facebook 7, 8, 18
fake Profiles 202
FAQs, MySpace 49, 203
Featured Artists 188
FeedBurner 116
56k modem 26
file formats 149
    AIFF 179
    animated GIF 151
    GIF 150
    JPEG 150
    LAME MP3 181
    MP3 128, 141, 171, 180
    MPEG-4 161
    PNG 150
    WAV 178
file size 152
Film, MySpace 118
filmmakers 118
find...
    classmates 81
    forums 106
    groups 105
    people 79, 81, 82
Firefox 33, 34, 80, 116
Flash 55
Flash Games 144
Flash Players 142
Flickr 155
flyers 188
forums 81, 103, 106, 118
FotoDunk 155
4-track 178
fraudsters 196
Friend Finder Filter 90
Friend ID 45, 146, 202, 205

Friends list 51, 78, 84
Friend Request 86, 87
Friends Reunited 6, 7, 19
Friendster 6, 7, 16, 125, 134, 147
Froogle 21

g

Games, MySpace 119
GarageBand 36, 178
GIF 150
GIMP 35, 151
Gmail 21, 30, 31, 85
Google 21, 165
Google Mail 21, 30, 31, 85
Google Reader 113
goths 126
graphic comments 98
grooming 38, 194
Grouper 17
Groups 81, 104, 142, 195
    Family & Home 60
    invites 105
    moderator 104
    Schools 81
    starting 105

h

haircuts 213
hacks 52, 135, 216
HAMSTERster 24
harassment 45, 203
Hatester 16
Hello page 67, 69
hexadecimal colour code 124, 126
hi5 22, 134
Hotmail 30, 85
Hotornot.com 156
hotspot 28
HTML 72, 97, 124, 146, 201

HTML links 98

i

"I Sing and Dance in My Car when
    Everyone Is Looking" 104
identity theft 44, 200, 202
IE 32
iLife 36
Illustrator 148
IM 20, 99
Image Dump 155
images 147
    hosts 154
    libraries 148
ImageShack 155
Imbee 24
iMovie HD 160
Infinite Teen Slang Dictionary, The 58
instant messaging 20, 99
Interests & Personality 71
Intermix Media 54
Internet Explorer 32
Introvertster 16
invitation-only networks 21
invites...
    friends 85
    guests 108
    link 85
iPhoto 35
iPod 160
IrfanView 153
iTunes 36, 160, 179, 180
iTunes-LAME 181

j

JPEG 150
junk email 93

k

keyboard shortcuts 71

l

LAME MP3 181
layout generators 131, 216
layouts, off-the-peg 134
Liberated Syndication 116
links 14, 89, 128
Linux 23
Listing Info 174
listings 118
logging in 74
logging out 74
Logic Express 36
login details 196
login screens 43

m

Mac 23, 26
Mail 86, 92
make...
    friends 83
    music 177
    video 158
malware 32
manage...
    calendar 110
    comments 96
    Friends list 89
    songs 137
Massively Multiplayer Online
    Role-Playing Game 23
MCPS-PRS 176
meeting people offline 197
Message Board 105
Microsoft 30, 32

MMORPG 23
Mobile Alerts 94
mobile phones 94, 158
movie trailers 119
Mozilla Foundation 33
MP3 128, 141, 171, 180
MP3 players 141, 175, 187
MPEG-4 161
Murdoch, Rupert 54
MuseNet 54
Music, MySpace 8, 118, 170, 183
   signing up 169
music
   downloading 170
   forums 187
   recording 178
   uploading 174
   videos 185
Music Settings 73, 137
My Pictures 147, 153
MyChingo 145
MySpace 14
   addiction 206
   Blogs 112
   Books 119
   Comedy 120
   Display Name 68
   Events 108
   Film 118
   history of 54
   homepage 61
   Music 8, 118, 170, 183
   Video 118
   whoring 78, 89
MySpaceBlog'r 114
MySpaceIM 100

n

name (MySpace Display Name) 71
netiquette 106
networking 73

newbies 123
News Corporation 54, 55
No Pic Forwarding 195
notes 95
notification emails 93

o

Odeo 116
off-the-peg layouts 134
offensive emails 93
online chat 102
online communities 3
open-source software 33
orkut 7, 21, 85
OS X Tiger 31, 33, 82
out-of-office message 75

p

paedophiles 9, 38, 194
PaintShop Pro 35
Pandora 17
Parents' Guide to MySpace 219
passwords 28, 63, 73, 201
PayPal 197
personal details 43
Petster 24
phishing 43, 196
Photobucket 165
Photo Ranking 156
photos 34, 147
   editing software 149
Photoshop 35
Picasa 21, 35
PicklePlayer 116
picture forwarding 195
Picture Policy 65
pimp your Profile 123
PNG 150
Podcasts 116

Podomatic 116
POP3 29
pornography 40
privacy 65, 70, 82, 195
Privacy Policy 64
Privacy Settings 74, 88, 99, 195
Private accounts 192, 194
Profile page
    boost your Profile 84
    fake Profiles 202
    pimp your Profile 123
    previewing your Profile 69
public-domain image libraries 148
public access 28

q

QuickTime 159, 161

r

Ranking Score 156
real-time messages 99
real-world encounters 197
Reaper 36, 178
remote server 30
remove comments 96
Report This Image 206
resolution 161
ResponseBase 54
RGB 126
RSS 20, 33, 113, 116

s

Safari RSS 33
Safe Mode 97, 176, 201
safeguards 40
safety tips 218
salutes 202

scams 196
Schools, MySpace 7, 72, 81, 120
sconex 19
scrollers 138
scrolling messages 138
search…
    for people 79
    for blogs 112
searchability 70, 73
search box 80
search tools 79
search widget 82
security 196
Service Pack 2 32
SignOut 74
sign-up process 62
six degrees of separation 79
SixDegrees.com 6
Skype 15
slang 58
slideshow 139
smilies 100
social networking 5, 6
source (view…) 58, 127
spam 93
speakers 179
special characters 72
stereo recording 178
stolen accounts 200
streaming 119, 163
subscribing to blogs 113
SubTags 146
surnames 88
syndication 116

t

tags 127
teachers 203
teal (duck) 129
technical problems 203

Terms of Service 64
text editor 71
threads 106
TinyPic 165
Top artists 186
Top books 119
Top Friends 89
Top Genres 56
Top Ranked 156
trackers 140
treble (EQ) 179
TypePad 17

u

Ultima Online 23
underage account holders 63
Uniform Resource Locator 67
Upcoming Shows 172
uploading…
    music 174
    pictures 64
URLs 67, 76
usage limits 27
user agreements 171

v

View All Friends 78
variable bit rate 182
verification of Friends Requests 64
Video, MySpace 118
video
    codes 166
    comments 98
    formats 161
    grabs 159
videocasts 116
viruses 196

visitor counters 138
vodcasts 116
volume levels 178

W

WAV 178
Web browser 32, 124
    Firefox 33, 34, 80, 116
    Internet Explorer 32
    MySpace as Home Page 70
Web search 79
webcam 158
Web images 151
weblog *see blogging*
webmail 30
webpage design 126, 133, 134
whoring, MySpace 78, 89
Whyville 24
Wi-Fi 28
Windows 31
Windows Movie Maker 160
Worst of MySpace 211

X

Xdrive 54

y

Yahoo! 31, 85
Yahoo! 360° 20, 155
YouTube.com 118, 157, 163

z

Zwinky 141

Listen Up!

"You may be used to the Rough Guide series being comprehensive, but nothing will prepare you for the exhaustive Rough Guide to World Music . . . one of our books of the year."

Sunday Times, London

ROUGH GUIDE MUSIC TITLES

Bob Dylan • The Beatles • Classical Music • Elvis • Frank Sinatra
Heavy Metal • Hip-Hop • iPods, iTunes & music online • Jazz
Book of Playlists • Opera • Pink Floyd • Punk • Reggae • Rock
The Rolling Stones • Soul and R&B • World Music Vol 1 & 2

BROADEN YOUR HORIZONS

ROUGH GUIDES

Rough Guides presents...

"Achieves the perfect balance between learned recommendation
and needless trivia" ***Uncut Magazine*** *reviewing Cult Movies*

Rough Guide Film & TV titles include:
American Independent Film • British Cult Comedy • Chick Flicks
Comedy Movies • Cult Movies • Gangster Movies • Horror Movies
Kids' Movies • Sci-Fi Movies • Westerns

BROADEN YOUR HORIZONS